THE OLYMPIC
CHRISTIAN

THE OLYMPIC CHRISTIAN

Comparing the benefits of two great events,
The Olympics and The Christian Race,
endorsing the benefits of the greater.

Richard A. Holder

Editor:
Doreen I. Fray

Cover Design:
G. D. Alejandra Martínez
www.alemtz.com

Printed in the UK by
CPI Group (UK) Ltd,
Croydon, CR0 4YY

First published in Great Britain in 2012
By Richard A.Holder
Email: pcholder@hotmail.com

The majority of biblical passages that are quoted in this book are quoted from *The King James Version*. Where there are exceptions to this application the abbreviations (CW) are used to indicate the use of *The Clear Word* Bible.

ISBN 978-0-9571460-0-6

THE OLYMPIC CHRISTIAN

ACKNOWLEDGEMENTS

The publication of my first book *The Power of a Double Portion* was a signification achievement; however the shortfalls of this fledgling writer were genially highlighted by encouraging readers. Many readers highlighted the virtues of the book despite its obvious shortfalls. Chief among the positive encouragers are such names Cleveland West Sr. and Gwendolyn Bramble. These and many more are pivotal to inspiring another attempt at writing a second edition. The success of *The Olympic Christian* is due also to the editorial assistance of Rosa Markham and Iris Walkinshaw. The encouragement of the members of The Holloway SDA Church has been instrumental to inspire the pursuit of excellence. I wish to encourage each reader to share the unique message of this book with at least three people. Many people will derive eternal benefits from the opportunity to become an Olympic Christian. Finally, during this critical hour when life has handed me the diagnosis of Adenocarcinoma of the Pancreas the support of my family has been immense. I wish to thank all for their tangible support and their prayers. May God be praised.

INTRODUCTION
The Origin of the Olympics

Originally founded in 776 BC in Olympia, the first Olympics lasted for 383 years until 393AD when it was abolished by the Roman Emperor Theodosius I. Ironically, due to his aversion for its pagan influence, Theodosius I, a Christian, abolished the games.[1] The one and only event of the original games was a 200-yard dash. This was the only event until a two stadia event was added in 724 BC and twenty four stadia events in 708BC.[2] The modern Olympics have grown to include twenty eight sports and three hundred and two events.

Whilst there is no evidence to indicate that Christians were active participants in the subsequent games, the Apostle Paul in a letter to the Corinthians indicates that Christians were observers and perhaps admirers of the contestants who pursued their quest to win the coveted first prize. According to history the victors in the original games were crowned with wreaths made from a sacred olive tree that grew behind the temple of Zeus.[3] It is ironic that the Apostle Paul recognised comparative virtues in games that were originally abolished by a Christian monarch for their alleged pagan influence.

In his observation and comparison of the contestants and their quest, the apostle demonstrates Christian pragmatism by alerting fellow believers to the similarities between the Christian and the Olympian. By this time it would appear that the sport of boxing had been an added event to the official games. In I Cor 9:24-27, Paul compares the Christian life to an athletic race and a boxer's competition. As the athletes in those original disciplines were trained and intensely focussed, likewise, the successful life of Christian demands that purpose, preparation and commitment be as competitive as the natural Olympian. The challenges and complexities of these mortal events are posted as comparative spiritual evaluation criterion, in order that the Christian may be aware that the spiritual application of preaching, witnessing or simply acquiring the name Christian, or the spiritual garb thereof, faces many challenges before the conclusion of the competition.

Thus, the Christian may grasp that, whilst he or she may not be a competitor in these modern Olympic games, there is a Para-Christian Olympic competition in constant progress. There are many experiences in the life of a practicing Christian that are compatible and comparable to the experiences of an Olympian. It is possible that all who participate in the Christian Olympics stand to achieve equally amazing feats. However, whilst it may be evident that they all can win, it must be equally evident that many can lose.

Thus, the Christian may compare and learn from the modern Olympian as he or she considers that, living lifestyle notwithstanding, he or she is an Olympic Christian.

1 THE COMPETITOR'S PREPARATION

Critical to the success of any athlete is the quality of their physical and mental preparation. On the XXIX Olympiad in Beijing, 204 countries committed a total of 11,028 athletes who competed in 28 sports and 302 events.[4] The magnitude of competition in today's Olympics is compounded by the vast scope of competitors, the intensity with which modern athletes prepare for their events, the heightened desire – due in part to possible publicity and monetary gain and the possibility of competing with athletes who are seasoned professionals.

Each athlete who enters the competitions does so with the expectation that he or she will derive some medal success from his or her pursued quest. As faint as the hope may be for the least competent performer, each competitor must present himself or herself as a credible competitor.

Personal Preparation

No matter how skilful or gifted an athlete may appear to be, the key to his or her success will depend upon the quality of the preparation. Training is an absolute must for today's' Olympic competitor.

In his guide for athletic success, Lance Smith informs the competitor that there must be a strategy for each section of the race. Smith points out that plans should cover the area of the athlete's strengths and weaknesses and the way to maximise every potential at every sector of the race.[5] Athletes, if possible, need to familiarise themselves with every sector of the race, planning tactics and alternative tactics for unexpected changes along the way. Knowledge and familiarisation of the course helps the athlete to decide and confirm his or her tactics for each sector of the race. Once the race has started the athlete's mind should be on each sector of the race.

Athletes should monitor themselves along every sector of the race, asking themselves a series of questions as they progress:

- How am I running?
- What is the position of my head?
- What is the position of my shoulders?
- How are my arms and hands flowing?
- How are my legs flexing?

These questions, and more, should reflect a series of questions that athletes should prepare to ask themselves as they pursue their course.

The Christian's Preparation

The Christian's life shares some comparisons with the lifestyle of an athlete. Whilst not entirely parallel in their lifestyles, there are many incentives for becoming a competitor in the Christian race. The ultimate reason for becoming a Christian athlete rests in the awarding of a prize that is far superior to that which can be achieved in human Olympic success. The Apostle Paul encourages every person to enter this race and become a Christian Olympiad. Two words reflect the scope of the invitation to become a Christian Olympiad; "*So Run*" (I Cor 9:24)!

The national and international Olympian gains entry into the competition due to the sponsorship of his or her respective countries. Thus, because of the selectivity of such candidacy as an Olympian, his or her success or failure will always have dual impact upon the person and upon the nation. The Christian Olympian, however, does not undergo any rigorous selection process. Everyone who has the capacity to hear, be mentally conscious, and understand the invitation, can immediately launch himself or herself into their candidacy for ultimate Olympic success. Whilst 11,028 selected candidates took part in the Beijing Olympics the invitation to take part in the Christian Olympics is unlimited and without bias or restriction.

The directive, "*so run*" (I Cor 9:24) is indeed a universal invitation that is reflected in the "*whosoever*" (Jn 3:16) invitation that is extended in the gospel of John. The open, universal, personal invitation that is extended to the conscious hearer is coupled with the guarantee of certain success if the individual completes the race. The guarantee of certain reward is reflected in the words -*"that ye may obtain"* (I Cor 9:24). The Clear Word Bible makes it plain to understand by stating: *"Everyone who runs in the Olympics gives it all he has, but only one person wins the laurel wreath.... But in the gospel race, everyone who runs faithfully and finishes is a winner"* (I Cor 9:24).

If winning is guaranteed to every Christian competitor, the focus of the competitor should not be consumed with the rank at the conclusion of the race, but on the capacity to finish the race. The statement of admonition given by the Apostle Paul at the close of his ministry and the end of his life, encourages the Christian Olympian to *"endure afflictions"* (II Tim 4:5). Equally important to the Christian Olympian, is understanding the consistency of the Apostle Paul who concluded his life's race with this statement of acclamation: *"I have fought a good fight, I have finished the course, I have kept the faith: Henceforth there is laid up for me a crown of righteousness"* (II Tim 4:7,8). Wrapped up within those final words are hints of the Christian Olympian's need for fitness and endurance.

Personal Fitness

Critical to the success of every athlete is the conditioning of the body for the respective discipline. The sprinter must train his or her body to maintain maximum capacity for speed. The long distant runner must train his or her body to endure time and distance. The boxer must train to maximise marksmanship accuracy, quickness to avoid being struck by his opponent and strength to endure to the final round. The weightlifter must train to maximise his or her capacity to lift the heaviest of weights that his or her weight class can endure. Thus, there is a fitness criterion for each athlete. The long distant runner cannot train like a weight lifter, neither should a horse rider train like a gymnast. Each Olympic event demands the respect of bodily preparation that is compatible to the possibility of success in that discipline.

As it is with the athlete, so must it be with the Christian. The Apostle spoke of the need for "*body subjection*" (I Cor 9:27).

There is a need and a demand for Christian discipline. The Olympic Christian must first understand some basic body dynamics. The body that we inhabit is not our independent possession to use as we please without the possibility of the penalty of both earthly and eternal consequences. Whether or not the athlete becomes a Christian Olympian or a non-Christian Olympian, the principle of body ownership remains the same. "*Know ye not that your body is the temple of the Holy Ghost....and ye are not your own*" (I Cor 6:19).

The human body is made of a complexity of blood, bones, nerves and tissues. A human body system is one of the most complex yet efficient systems found on the earth. The main organs of a normal person are kidneys, heart, lungs, brain and spinal cord. All these organs are the basic building blocks of the human body system and every other body part or organ is related to these organs in one way or another. The functioning of every organ is different from, but is inter-related with each other and works together by co-ordinating with each other. The human body is divided into four major categories, namely the Circulatory, Digestive, Immune and Nervous Systems.[6] It is the apparent normality of these systems that enable the athlete to compete on an equal level with his or her competitor in the major Olympics. Athletes whose body systems are regarded as deficient are given the privilege to compete against each other in the Paralympics.

Central to the performance of every system is the human brain. This complex mass of jelly- like fat, weighs approximately three pounds and consists of 100 billion nerve cells. This mass of complexity is the organ that makes us human. It is this organ that gives people the capacity for creativity, language, moral judgments, rational thought, and athleticism. It is also responsible for each individual's personality, memories, movements and how we perceive the world.[7] It is the principle organ that enables and empowers every athlete.

How dynamic, vast, and amazing are the accomplishments of the human athlete? With practice and extreme training, the athlete is able to somersault through the air, plummet water like a fish, wriggle, waggle, leap and twist acrobatically on land. It is no wonder that King David expressed his admiration to God with the words; "*I will praise thee; for I am fearfully and wonderfully made: marvellous are thy works*" (Ps 139:14).

The Christian Church is one body system comprised of many units. The Church is compared to a biological body system. "*For as we have many members in one body, and all members have not the same office. So being many, we are one body in Christ, and every one a member of one another*" (Rom 12:4,5). As the limbs of the body co-ordinate and co-operate to enhance the body's performance, so the Christian is encouraged to observe the comparison and apply practical lessons. The sole organ that bears responsibility for the coordination of all systems is the brain.

Whilst the human body is made up of blood, muscles, bones, ligaments and nerves, the nervous system serves the body in the most vital role as the body's centre for communications and electrical-chemical wiring network. The Nervous System is a key homeostatic regulatory and coordinating system, detecting, interpreting and responding to changes in internal and external conditions. The nervous system integrates countless bits of information and generates appropriate reactions by sending electrochemical impulses through nerves to effector organs such as muscles and glands.[8]

The word homeostatic addresses itself to the body's state of equilibrium. The equilibrium needs of the Olympian and the Christian are similar. Both Olympians need emotional stability – a mental state of calmness and composure, bodily balance – a physical state or sense of being able to maintain body stability, chemical balance – a state in which all forces or systems of the body are in balance, and situational balance – a state of awareness of opposing factors, and the need for bodily, social, or psychological adjustment. Technically speaking, the human brain is the most dynamic computer on earth, being able to compute complex information and relay informational needs to the appropriate body system.

The scope and aggressiveness of modern competitions are extremely great. The possibility to excel and be triumphant is measured in fractions of a second. Imagine, therefore, the intensity that is injected into years of preparation for a sprinter in pursuit of ten seconds of performance in the Olympic stadium. The statistics from the Beijing Olympics are staggering. The cost of a $500 million stadium with the capacity to accommodate 100,000 spectators is a far cry from the humble setting of the first Olympics. This modern venue is the arena that is constructed to accommodate the gifted competitor. In the case of the sprinter, $500 million is invested in order to witness the demonstration of ten seconds of physiological speed.

There is a direct correlation between the athletic capability of an individual athlete and the brain power that motivates performance. The brain is the organ comprised of soft nervous tissue which fills the cranium. The mind, on the other hand, is the element of a person that enables them to be aware of their environment and thus react and respond to the circumstances that tend to lead to successful performances. Whereas the judges and spectators are left to draft their assumptions of the state of mind of the athlete during and after their competition, the monitoring of the mind of the Christian Olympian is subject to a far higher erudite and instantaneous divine mechanism, the Holy Spirit. Whilst the measure of the performance of the Olympian is a temporary periodic assessment of the quality of his or her mind-set, the assessment of the Christian's mind-set endures until the expiry of natural life. Thus, whilst the modern Olympian is subject to a momentary analysis of their athletic performance, the Christian Olympian is subject to a lifetime analysis.

Preparing the Mind

After the successful defence of their National Basketball Association title in 2010, Ron Artest, the small forward/shooting guard for the Los Angeles Lakers publicly thanked his doctor for assisting his mental preparation for the games. In their quest to remain focussed on the moment of competition and due to the intimidating influences of formidable competitors, titanic and noisy spectators and electronic monitoring systems, certain Olympians have reportedly applied the assistance of neurotherapy. In an era when winning means far more than securing the presentation of a humble garland, athletes prepare themselves not just for athletic success, but for the possible inflow of financial endorsements that ensue thereafter. Therefore, the stakes of competing in modern Olympics are measured by the possible size of financial endorsements that accrue after the competition.

The Christian is urged to be more vigilant. Solomon gave the counsel; *"Keep thy heart with all diligence; for out of it are the issues of life"* (Prov 4:23). The use of the word heart in this context of Christian terminology encompasses the broad application of the mind. The use of the word *"issues,"* similarly broad in its application, alludes to a lengthy list of prohibited behavioural practices for the Christian. Whilst Solomon was more general in his identification of the productions of the heart, Jesus was more specific in His identification of possible hindrances to the Christian's Olympic performance.

The issues identified by Jesus highlight a list of behavioural practices that are prohibited in social interaction but He also included one prohibition against the Godhead. The list of behavioural practices toward humanity includes a prohibition of evil thoughts, murders, adulteries, fornication, thefts, and false witnessing (Matt 15:19). The engagement of these practices is stipulated as defiling practices. It is evident that Jesus' list first included a prohibition of evil thoughts. The implication of this inclusion highlights the startling awareness that the Olympic Christian is subject to perpetual neuro-analysis. As Olympians are assigned track positions respective to the race that they have entered and must retain their positions to avoid disqualification, so must Christians adhere to their prescribed lifestyle in order to avoid a negative conclusion to an ambitious commitment.

There is a track that is defined for the Christian. This track is narrow and prescriptive. The reason for the prescription is not to deprive the Christian of any personal joy but it is to enhance the development of personal virtues that will qualify and enable the Christian to benefit from heaven's eternal habitation. Heaven is a place of beauty, wealth and virtue. Those who are privileged to finish their Olympic course will be those who have already embraced a spirit of honesty, justice, purity, loveliness, and a good report from their fellow citizens. The Christian Olympian will, therefore, only qualify to inhabit a resident in heaven when the internal character is cleared of all heavenly prohibitions.

The brain is the seat of intelligence of the individual. It is from the brain that all thoughts and actions derive. Whilst Jesus declared that it is not what goes into a man's belly that defiles a man, but what comes out of the heart, there is one exception of a defiling element that remains within. The average post-modern mind is familiar with the term, virtual reality. Whist virtual reality is defined as a computer generated environment that simulates three dimensional realities; the practice of environmental simulation is not exclusive to this post-modern age. As far back as 594 BC, God was explaining to His prophets the secret practice of virtual reality in the lives of His ancient leaders.

In a startling dialogue with the Prophet Ezekiel, in vision, the Lord justified His action to allow His people to go into Babylonian captivity by revealing to Ezekiel the practices that were being simulated in the brain. In a startling revelation, the Lord declared to Ezekiel; "*Son of Man, hast thou seen what the ancients of Israel do in the dark, every man in the chambers of his imagery? For they say, The Lord seeth us not, the Lord hath forsaken us*" (Ezek 8:12). Furthermore, the Lord proceeded to describe the sins that were being harboured in the mind, unseen to the naked eye. It was for their addiction to idol worship and many more abominations that the Lord permitted the invasion and subjugation of the nation of Israel.

One of the chief abominations cited by the Lord was the practice of virtual reality sinning. The ancients of Israel were at ease with their neurological abominations, unaware of the fact that they were not shielded from the scrutiny of divine gaze. To the uncircumcised mind, it would appear that the Lord is intrusive in His invasion of the thoughts of a man or woman;

however, the actions of an individual are commenced in his or her thoughts. King Solomon was therefore correct when he stated that, as a man thinks in his heart, so is he. It is generally considered that thought determines action, action determines character, and character determines destiny.

The primary reason for the profound scrutiny of human thought is to measure the degree of unpretentious sincerity that a person professes. There will be no masquerades in heaven. The primary reason for the open disclosure of divine monitoring is to inform the individual that quality of inner thinking is a priority issue for the Christian Olympian and especially so since the Lord has declared that every action performed by each individual will be considered in their final judgement. *"For God shall bring every work into judgement, with every secret thing, whether it be good, or whether it be evil"* (Ecc 12:1).

Seeing then that every aspect of our lives will be brought under the scrutiny of divine analysis, Peter asked the question; *"What manner of persons ought we to be in all holy conversation and godliness"* (II Pet 3:11)? In this era of information bombardment and overload, it is almost impossible to shield the mind from unholy influences. The aim of the Christian, however, is to run the race without succumbing to prohibited distractions. Hence the admonition to keep the heart with all diligence, thereby, shielding it from any negative influences that would thwart the progress or success of the Olympian.

Admonition once again comes to the Christian from the Apostle Paul in his letter to the Philippians. *"Let this mind be in you"* (Phil 2:5). Jesus actively demonstrated that His mind was focussed on a vital mission that reflected the will of His Father. Whilst Paul's letter to the Philippians states that He Jesus *"made himself* of no reputation,"* he was referring to the fact that Jesus' ministry avoided ostentation. It was a ministry that humbly reflected the will of His Father. *"For I came down from heaven, not to do mine own will, but the will of him that sent me"* (Jn 6:38). This was evidently reflected in His mentality, as early as age twelve. This statement was made to His earthly parents; *"Wist ye not that I must be about my Father's business"* (Lk 2:49)? In constant recognition of His objective focus, He Himself often reflected on the reality that His *"hour had not yet come."*

That mind-set was aware of both time and symbolism, therefore He did not deviate from purpose, but was faithful and resilient amidst the bombardments of ridicule, enticement, betrayal, persecution, and crucifixion. One of the symbolisms for wine in the New Testament is the representation of blood. When Mary the mother of Jesus drew his attention to the fact that the supply of wine had been exhausted, it was, inadvertently, a call for His blood. His reply was; *"woman, what have I to do with thee? Mine hour has not yet come"* (Jn 2:4).

In contrast, however, when Philip and Andrew informed Him that certain men of Greek origin were requesting to speak with

Him, His reply was; *"the hour is come that the Son of man should be glorified"* (Jn 12;23). When the devil was in the heaves of launching his final attacks against Him, Jesus said to His disciples; *"the prince of this world cometh and hath nothing in me"* (Jn 14:30). Whilst the testimony of His troubled spirit declared, *"one of you shall betray me"* (Matt 26:53), yet He did not deviate from the path of His impending doom. Twelve thousand and more angels were at His disposal[31] to prevent His arrest and crucifixion yet He did not succumb to the temptation. With His disciples in total disarray, He trod the winepress alone. In His final moments of death He even took the time to utter; *"Father, forgive them for they know not what they do"* (Lk 23:34).

Jesus was a man who drew on the strength that was available through His Father. By so doing He has demonstrated that the same strength is available to anyone who will set their mind to run the race to its completion. Many are the distractions that confront the contemporary Christian. The magnitude and multiplicity of distractions are in proportional contrast to the vast prize that is available. The possibility to succeed and gain the coveted eternal prize is in contrast to the magnitude of the loss that is already suffered by the demonic forces who have no possibility to regain any heavenly residence.

The Olympic Christian is blessed with a grand and auspicious opportunity. The possibility to enter heaven eternally is within the grasp of every individual. Whilst the traps, hindrances and temptations are myriad, the Christian has been given the assurance that Divine assistance is more that equal to the challenges that entice and ensnare. It is, by no means a completion without obstacles and deliberate hindrances. The encouragement to run the race has come from the Apostle Paul who, as a non-competitor, witnessed the calibre of Jesus as He ran the race and then having later made the decision to join the race, joyfully completed despite formidable interferences and punishments.

The lives of these two individuals, Jesus and Paul, represent two contrasting spectrums of an individual's capacity to join the race and realise its successful completion. Jesus gave up His place in the realm of ecstasy that we all desire to inhabit. He forsook the habitation of the heavenly host and became a living model of success in the midst of demonic sponsored opposition. *"And being found in fashion as a man, he humbled Himself and became obedient unto death, even the death of the cross"* (Phil 2:8).

As a result of His successful completion of the race, He received the eternal accolade from His Father and the invitation to resume His place in the heavenly realm. The prize that awaited Jesus was not a humble garland but the crown reserved for the King of Kings and Lord of Lords. He became highly exalted by His Father and thus delivers to each competitor a profile for successful completion of the Christian race and the incentive for the prize that awaits.

The life of Apostle Paul was a life in direct contrast. His experience derived from a life of Pharisaic pride, arrogance, violence and persecution. The transition from his former persuasion to the life of a committed Christian Olympian was confrontational. He was a sceptic who came in direct contact with the object of his scepticism and dramatically became a believer. While on another journey to spearhead the continuation of a Jewish vendetta to persecute and annihilate Jewish converts to Christianity, he himself was confronted by an irresistible spiritual force. As he drew near to the city of Damascus, a beam of light from heaven shone directly upon him and an ensuing voice asked the question; *"Saul, Saul, why are you persecuting me"* (Acts 9:4 CW)?

When he enquired about the identity of the voice, he received an amazing, life transforming reply. *"I am Jesus, the One you are persecuting. You've been fighting against the pricks of your own conscience ever since you consented to Stephen's death, and you have been taking out your anger on my people"* (Acts 9:5 CW).

The experience of Paul on the Damascus Road is symptomatic of every spiritual life changing experience. The decision to enter the Christian race is first initiated by a message to the brain from the Lord of our brain. Emotional exuberance may be the external celebration of a cerebral realisation and commitment. The Christian Olympian cannot compete solely on the adrenaline of emotional ecstasy. There must be a message that penetrates the cerebral cortex of the brain. This critical area processes perception, sensations, learning, reasoning, memory, and the analysis of sensory information.[9] Mere emotional awareness is not sufficient to sustain the Christian Olympian through the endless emotional bombardment that the brain would encounter before completing the race. Thus, like Paul each individual must come to an intellectual awareness of who he or she is in contrast to who Jesus is.

There must be the awareness that Jesus is Lord. The task of making everyone aware of Jesus as Lord is the principle purpose of the gospel. Matthew stated that the gospel shall be preached to the world (Matt 24:14), and John specified that the world included every nation, kindred, tongue and people (Rev 14:6). The scope of this global message is an open invitation that encourages and makes it possible for everyone to become a Christian Olympian.

The power of the gospel to achieve its task, resides in the potency of its message, the divine force that energises and empowers the message and the positive response of the hearer. The uncompromised message of the gospel is moral and deferential. The thrust of its message aims to inform the sinner of the ultimate unprofitable lifestyle outside the experience of being a Christian Olympian and the benefits that are to be realized when a person commits his or herself to the divine management of God, their Creator.

The gospel message covers a broad scope of panoramic issues. Nevertheless, it possesses the remarkable ability to be personal and microscopic. It is a roadmap for humanity's moral code of behaviour, yet it also possesses the remarkable ability to influence the profound conscience of each individual. "*For the word of God is quick and powerful, and sharper than any two edged sword, piercing even to the dividing of the joints and the marrow, and is a discerner of the thoughts and intents of the heart*" (Heb 4:12).

Paul was not yet in the race, but the voice that spoke to him during his enlightening encounter with destiny, asked a profound question; "*Why are you fighting against the pricks?*" The lesson of Paul's confrontational experience unveils a basic pattern of experience that confronts every non-believer of the Christian race. The lesson is that each individual experiences a pinhole perforated impression of a conscience changing message. Hence it is as a prick.

The central cortex of the human brain is uniquely designed and equipped to accept and analyse the prick of a message. Paul, the voice declared, was the object of many pricks. Could it be that for those who refuse to yield to the impressions of a conscience changing message, there awaits the high possibility of a confrontational Damascus experience? Is it not more convenient to receive and accept the pricks of the gospel?

The direct divine confrontation that transformed the thinking of Paul is the same force that spoke to Elijah in a *"still small voice"* (I Kg 19:14). The application of the still small voice is more commonly experienced universally than the direct confrontation. Nevertheless, the contrasting ranges of conscience pricking messages are designed to convince the receiver of the benefits of being a Christian Olympian.

Paul was a contemptuous assassin for the opposition, yet he yielded to the supremacy of the divine messenger by asking the question; *"Lord, what do you want me to do"* (Acts 9:6)? The reply to his question and his subsequent remarkable transformation resulted in a convert that has become the most prolific writer in the New Testament.

It is the impact of Paul's dramatic conversion and his invitation to join the Christian race that adds to the credibility of a Christian Olympian. Running the race was an objective lesson of commitment and determination amidst the most formidable opposition and unscrupulous interference. Paul received punishment from both Romans and Jews. On five occasions he received thirty-nine lashes from Jewish opposition and three times was beaten with rods by the Romans. On one occasion he was dragged out of town, beaten and stoned by a mob. He suffered the discomfort of three shipwrecks and was in danger of losing his life to floods, robbers, and idol worshipers. The extent of his missionary exploits often found him tired, hungry and exhausted (II Cor 11::24-27).

With such a tirade of vitriol against him, he could have grown despondent and given up the race, nevertheless, he regarded himself as chief of sinners. (I Tim 1:5) The legacy of his books enables the post-modern reader to benefit from the positives of his personal experience and take the decision to plunge into the Christian race.

Many would have capitulated under the pressure of satanic opposition; however he withstood the test and ran a successful race. It is due to his insatiable desire to write that we are benefited by his invitation and encouragement. Being transformed from Saul- the dedicated persecutor of the early disciples of Jesus, to a dedicated apostle of Jesus, the newly transformed Paul joined a race that enabled him to set new Christian Olympic records. There are twenty-seven books in the New Testament, thirteen (48%) of which are attributed to the writings of the Apostle Paul. His commitment to a change in lifestyle was due to the traumatic encounter that convicted him to stop fighting against the life changing messages, the pricks. On that eventful day, he heard more than a voice. He received and understood the message and he yielded to the invitation of the Messenger. That was a message that beamed directly from the throne room of heaven, and he did indeed see the light. No pun intended.

Preparing the Eye

The eye is a remarkable photographic instrument that enables the body to capture an accurate image of its surroundings. It is indeed a remarkable camera, and when connected to the brain they combine to form a dynamic information databank and data processing system. Through the auspices of what the eye sees, the brain is able to capture a photographic image of shapes, colours and dimensions by processing the light they reflect or emit. The human eye is therefore significantly responsible for visualizing the life transforming message of the gospel, both optically and mentally. While this remarkable photographic instrument is able to capture the beautiful images of life, equally it is also capable of capturing images that are distracting to the soul.

Whilst the eye is remarkable for the images it captures, the brain must develop an equal capacity to accurately analyse the captured images. Despite the evidence of Paul's education and intense dedication to Judaism, his testimony reveals how misguided a person can be about their self-confidence to be saved. "*If anyone could have confidence in himself to earn salvation, I certainly could. I was circumcised an Israelite from the tribe of Benjamin when I was eight years old. I grew up and was trained in the strictest Pharisaic tradition. If there ever was a real Hebrew I was one. I kept the Jewish laws so well that I was made a member of the Sanhedrin, the Jewish National Council. Sincere? Was I ever! In fact, I was so sincere that the Sanhedrin in Jerusalem entrusted me with the responsibility to rid the country of Christians. As far as external conformity to the law was concerned, I was blameless. I once thought that all these external things would save me, but now I know that they're worthless"* (Phil 3:4-7CW).

What made the difference to such a dedicated Pharisee? It was the dramatic encounter with new light and enlightenment. Firstly, the bright light of Jesus' appearance of the Damascus Road assaulted his optical vision and resulted in temporary blindness. The fact that he then needed the assistance of a sighted person to help him on his way caused him to reflect upon his personal and spiritual outlook on life.

Secondly, the experience of being dramatically confronted by the person whose disciples he had opposed, and the realisation that Jesus was indeed a powerful God , caused him to engage in a swift mental analysis of his personal mortality. By asking two significant questions, *"Who art thou, Lord?"* and *"What wilt thou have me to do?"* Paul conceded that there was a power that was superior to Roman and Jewish authorities.

Thirdly, the brief instructions from Jesus that became the prelude to the renewal of his sight and his baptism within days rather than months, were evidence that the new light entered his system with threefold impact.

The presentation of the gospel in written form allows the reader to experience the thoughts and the voice of God. The law of God was available in written format for all to read and adhere, however, it lacked sufficiency to supply the reader with visual empowerment. The word of God is likened unto a lamp and a light, "*a lamp for my feet and a light for my path*" (Ps 119:105CW). The power of the written word was boosted when God allowed His Son to be born in the likeness of human flesh. The application and usage of the word "*word*" is both general and specific when applied to the written Bible and the Son of God. The Bible is the written word of God, but Jesus is also referred to as "*the Word.*"

"*In the beginning was the Word, and the Word was with God, and the Word was God. The same was in the beginning with God*" (Jn 1:1,2). "*And the Word became flesh and dwelt among us, and we beheld his glory, the glory of the only begotten Father, full of grace and truth*" (Jn 1:14). In Psalms 119 the written word is referred to as an illuminating agent for the benefit of physical ambulation but in the book of John the noun "*word*" is referring to the Son of God who became visible in order that we may have a clearer mental vision of the person and salvational worth of God. Whilst the word is written for the purpose of illuminating the person of the Son of God, Paul openly declared that there was a period in his life when he could not see the "*WORD*" even though he was an avid student of the "*word.*" This was a tragic spiritual visual impairment which resulted in the pursuance of a vocation that simply led him down the wrong path. He was among the multitude that has eyes but could not see. Jesus expressed their spiritual dilemma with the statement: *"The light shone in darkness but the darkness comprehended it not"* (Jn 1:5).

It is possible for a person with excellent academic qualifications to lack a dynamic understanding of the gospel. The rationale for such conclusion is that *"spiritual things are spiritually discerned"* (I Cor 2:14). It is the purpose of God, through the agency of the Holy Spirit, to bring every individual to the point and place of optical spiritual enlightenment. The natural world, as we visualize it, is not capable of leading an individual to a state of spiritual enlightenment. This process is only possible with the assistance of God, hence He said; *"I will instruct thee in the way which thou shalt go: I will guide thee with mine eye"* (Ps 32:8).

The guidance of God is necessary in order to instruct and constrain the eye from reckless vision. The natural eye is never satisfied with seeing, (Ecc 1:8) and is most likely to perpetually gaze at those things that are hazardous to the soul. The biblical language speaks of the wandering eye as an offensive eye. *"If thy right eye offend thee, pluck it out"* (Matt 18:9). The Christian Olympian is therefore confronted with the challenge to restrain his or her eyes from gazing upon those scenes that will influence the onset of moral corrosion.

The challenge that confronts each non-Christian is the same dilemma that confronted Saul. He was intelligent and sincere in his beliefs, but he was sincerely running on the wrong spiritual track. He was the leader of a group of blind Pharisaical dogmatists. Under his leadership, they pursued Jewish converts to Christianity with the intention of bringing them to trial and execution. When Stephen, the first Christian martyr, was stoned to death, witnesses laid down their clothes at the feet of a young man whose name was Saul (Acts 7:58). After his conversion to Christianity he later changed his name from Saul to Paul. In as much as the Pharisees were ardent and zealous for their Judaism, they were sincerely blinded in their zeal. *"If the blind lead the blind, both shall fall into the ditch"* (Matt 15:14).

Paul did not realise that he was spiritually blind until he was confronted by Jesus whilst on the road to Damascus. Two significant occurrences were transformational. The first was the sound of the voice that asked; *"Why are you persecuting me?"* The second was the bright light that inflicted temporary blindness. Immediately after the fall and the bright light, his eyes were opened but he could see no man (Acts 9:27). Paul suffered temporary blindness for the duration of three days. Within those three days another visionary transformation took place in the life of another devout Christian, named Ananias who expressed his inability to conceive Saul as a newly converted brother.

In a move to facilitate the conversion of Saul and due to his inability to see the transformation, the Lord spoke to Ananias, a local convert in Damascus by means of a vision. A spiritual vision is an act of cognitive communication from the Lord to a particular individual, occurring either during his or her hours of sleep or in the hour of consciousness. The experience itself renders the individual in a coma-like state, unable to interact with his or her human surroundings, yet fully alert in of his or her mental and spiritual transformation. Thus, a person who has been the recipient of a vision is able to recall and record their ecstatic experience. Therefore, when the Lord spoke to Ananias in vision, Ananias was confident of the message because of the validity of the Messenger. It was a visionary experience for all.

If we could utilise the simulation of the Olympic track, on one hand, it would demonstrate that Saul could see physically, but on the other hand, he was off track spiritually. Consequently, Ananias could see physically and spiritually, therefore he was on track spiritually but limitations in his spiritual vision prohibited him from seeing the possible transformation that would place such a heretic as Paul on track. Immediately after Saul's conversion he was on track and could see spiritually, but was he physically blind.

There are many lessons to be learnt from these two experiences. The vision of one who is not an Olympic Christian is limited unless and until the Lord delivers a vision changing experience. The assistance of those who are Christian Olympians may be pivotal to the progress of those who are newcomers to the race. However, if the potential helper is also limited in vision, it will demand the help of the Lord to anoint the eyes of both in order that they may both benefit from being Christian Olympians. The Lord assisted the vision of Ananias by showing him the future worth of Paul towards the entire Christian race. Ananias' vision led him to lay holy hands on Paul; *"And immediately there fell from his eyes as it had been scales, and he received his sight forthwith, and arose and was baptized"* (Acts 9:18).

Both spiritual and natural vision are pivotal to the transition and growth of the natural person into an Olympic Christian. Where there is a lack of vision the people perish. Indeed there are many who perish due to their lack of vision. Many suffer from spiritual deficiencies that are compatible to the natural optical visual deficiencies. Many have a form of visual deficiency known as myopia. Those who suffer from myopia are short-sighted in the application of spiritual sight. They are able to see events that are local, but they exercise little capacity to see heavenly issues afar off. Such Christians may be busy addressing the needs of social issues in the areas of philanthropy and volunteer charity.

The coming of the Lord and the fulfilment of prophesies are not items on their spiritual radar. Some suffer from hyperopia and these are spiritual visionaries, they are the opposite of myopic Christians. They can see the impact and importance of heavenly issues very clearly. They are competent to interpret prophetic issues and have a clear understanding of eschatological event. However, these prophetic visionaries are of little practical benefit. Of these, it may be said, that they are so heavenly minded that they are of no earthly good. It is possible that many who will be condemned according to the description of Matt 7:21-23 will be those who are afflicted with spiritual hyperopia.

Myopia and hyperopia represent extreme opposites. Therefore, there is a majority of spiritually deficient individuals who fall between these extremes. The natural eye is regarded as carnal in its capacity, full of adultery (II Pet 2:14) and lust (I Jn 2:16). However, the Lord is willing and able to be the spiritual optician. His counsel to all is to secure from Him the eyesalve that is sufficient to cure anyone of his or her spiritual deficiency and enable them to discern the things of God (Rev 3:18). It is common for a non-Christian to declare that he or she can neither see nor understand spiritual issues. The promise to all who desire to become a Christian Olympiad is that, the same Jesus that assisted the transformation of Saul, is able and willing to assist in the transformation that facilitates spiritual enlightenment.

Notes

1. Jenifer Rosenburg, <u>History of the Olympics</u>. About.com
2. Nostos Hellenic Information Society UK,
   <u>Brief History of the Olympic Games</u>.
3. Nostos.
4. Wikipedia, <u>The Free Encyclopedia</u>. 2008 Summer Olympics.
5. L. Smith, <u>How to Prepare for your next Competition</u>.
   Brian McKenzie's Successful Coaching (ISSN 1745-7513), Issue 33. 2006.
6. htxtp://www,righthealth.com/topic/<u>TheHumanBodySystem/overview</u>/uc_
   kosmixarticles#xzz19gDufulUx
7. National Geographic.com: <u>Brain</u>
8. Body Guide, <u>Powered by Adam</u>. Adam.com
9. Arthur C. Guyton, *Textbook of Medical Psysiology*. W.B.Saunders Company.
   Philadelphia. London. Toronto. Fifth Edition. 1976: p:743-757.

2 VISIONS OF TRANSFORMATION

The need, application and effect of spiritual eye salve was wonderfully demonstrated in the life and experiences of Paul. He was highly commended by his contemporaries and for his fidelity to the cause of the Sanhedrin, yet spiritually, he was a very blind man. He fitted into the category of those who have eyes but see not and ears yet hear nothing. Paul needed the application of spiritual eyesalve but he was not cognizant of the need to volunteer for its application. His experience on the road to Damascus led him headlong into a confrontational experience with God which resulted in the realization of both spiritual and natural blindness.

Paul was a devout and learned Pharisee, yet when he was knocked to the ground he asked a very basic question; *"Who art thou Lord"* (Acts 9:5)? How is it possible that a person could harness significant and commendable learning from the Word of God, yet had no acquaintance with the God of the word? The simple answer is also revealed in Paul's Damascus experience. It is possible for a reader to cultivate a forensic grasp and appreciation for the text of the gospel, but until he or she has a one to one communication with the Lord of the gospel, he or she will never know who God is. Without such knowledge the reader will remain in spiritual darkness.

Whilst at the height of his experience as a Pharisee Paul was unaware of his spiritual blindness, but amazingly, when he was rendered physically blind; spiritual vision ensued from his terse conversation with the Lord. The resultant experiences of fear, trembling, astonishment and interrogatory conversation highlighted, to himself, the need of elevated spiritual sight and understanding that superseded the teachings of the Pharisees. The awareness of his need initiated immediate proactivity.

The quality of a person's spiritual experience will be directly proportionate to his/her spiritual proactivity. The Pharisees relentlessly pursued Jesus throughout His ministry and despite the testimony of the excellence of His words, *"never man spake like this man"* (Jn 7:46). they did not experience the effect of spiritual conversion. Saul, their chief advocate, was the recipient of two statements from Jesus that immediately ensued a change in thought, a change in name, a change in lifestyle, and a change in behaviour. Spiritual ignorance preceded his conversion but as soon as he received his dramatic enlightening, he followed his enlightenment with the positive commitment of baptism.

Spiritual ignorance is an obstacle to proactive spiritual behaviour. Individuals whose anti-Christian behaviour is precipitated by their ignorance of spiritual issues, are beneficiaries of God's unmerited grace and forgiveness. God winks. (Acts 17:30) When a light of acknowledgement is shone upon them, they automatically lose their previous divine immunity. Therefore, when a person is credited with the knowledge of who God is, that person is given the freedom to accept or reject the enlightenment. Rejection of divine knowledge is a declaration of his/her refusal to join the Christian race. Acceptance of the knowledge of God's existence and Lordship is a provisional decision to enter the Christian race but must be confirmed by baptism.

The application of the rite of Baptism in the New Testament was made prominent by John the Baptist who preached a vibrant message of repentance and baptism. *"John did baptize in the wilderness, and preach the baptism of repentance for the remission of sins"* (Mk 1:4). Preaching is a theological discourse that God has employed to inform the human race of the dangers of sin and the need and opportunity for spiritual renewal. Preaching is basically a form of dramatized teaching.

Throughout history humanity has demonstrated that individuals are captivated by dramatized presentations. The excellence of sermonic delivery is reflected in the academic preparation and animated delivery of the presenter. The quality of a good sermon may be rated from the range of shallowness to eloquence and profundity. It may be that a preacher who demonstrates a lack of preparation and or mental dexterity, is able to command and sustain a huge audience, whilst an individual of profound learning and preparation is only able to maintain a scattering of listeners. The phenomenon is known as *"the foolishness of preaching"* (I Cor 1:21).

The vast proliferation of books and the expansion of complex technology testify to the enormous wisdom of mankind, yet the wisdom of the world does not present itself as a facilitator for learning about God. *"People can understand Him sufficiently if they only watch His power and divine attributes at work in nature. It has been that way since the creation of this world. So they have no excuse for what they are doing. Although they could see God at work in nature, they still did not give Him credit for his marvellous acts, nor were they thankful for His blessings. They became arrogant and proud of their learning, and their foolish hearts were darkened. They thought they were brilliant, but actually they were fools. In attempting to fashion an image of the glorious, eternal God, they tried to make Him look like some Roman hero or like a god as half man and half goat, or even like some birds or creeping things"* (Rom 1:20CW).

Whereas the world has a vast supply of erudite professors and scholars who have perfected the skills of micro analysis, yet *"it has pleased God by the foolishness of preaching to save them that believe, because the foolishness of God is wiser than men"* (I Cor 1:25). God has employed the simplicity of preaching to convey the message that there is eternal merit in being a Christian Olympian.

There is eternal merit in running the Christian race, no matter what may be your current mental, physical, or religious persuasion.

The purpose of a biblical preacher is to make plain the reason and benefits for becoming an Olympic Christian. Thus, John the Baptist preached a message of repentance and remission. Someone may have experienced the misfortune to listen to a preacher who did not take his or her responsibility seriously and have listened to a misguided or false message. If you are such an individual, let me remind you that the purpose of preaching is to make the message of repentance and remission absolutely clear. Eternal salvation is not a myth, neither is the need of remission to be considered carelessly.

God desires for everyone to hear, understand and accept His message of salvation; however He does not employ supernatural leverage of assigning angels to perform the task of divine heralds. God uses the auspices of human preachers and through those preachers He appeals to the intelligent understanding of the hearer. The process is logical and simple.

The legitimate preaching of the gospel is an appeal to listeners to hear, understand and accept the wisdom and transforming power of the spiritual change process. The Word of God is a spiritual change agent. When the Word is appropriately processed in the brain, it produces a response of faith in the word and faith in the God of the word. When faith is activated in the brain, there is an immediate invisible commencement of a transfer of righteousness from Jesus Christ, the source of our righteousness to the person who believes by faith. No one is born into this world as a believer. Belief in the word of God comes as a result of hearing the word of God. Due to the fact that the word of God provides a description of what is possible for the reader or listener, there must be an enactment of belief through faith.

If belief is the document that contains a description of the treasures of all that is possible for the believer, then faith is the password that opens the document. The capacity to believe in the word of God is evident in a person's ability to think; no matter how minimal may be the measurement of their dynamic thinking. The application of belief and the activation of faith are only possible when an individual hears the Word. The question is then asked; *"How shall they hear without a preacher"* (Rom 12:3)?

For the sake of our understanding of the transfer or delivery of spiritual information, preaching and teaching are considered as equal postmen. Whoever delivers the word is considered as having beautiful feet (Rom 10:15). Every individual that is born on this earth is gifted with a measure of faith (Rom 12:3). However, that faith has to be activated in order to access and make sense of the document. *"Faith cometh by hearing, and hearing by the word of God"* (Rom 10:17). This therefore is the appeal both of this book and the appeal of the Word of God; Join the Christian race, be a Christian Olympian, and run the race to the end.

In as much as there are many who refuse to become a Christian Olympian due to their blatant and stubborn decision to abstain from entering the race, there are many who express apprehension due to negative reflections of their spiritual fitness to compete and endure. It is possible that an insight in to the meaning of the word *"remission"* may assist someone to be released from their apprehensions. John the Baptist preached a message of repentance and remission. Repentance can be likened to a train and remission likened to the reduction in distance as the train meanders and winds its way to the terminus. The presence of sin and the impact of its intrusion into human life is the greatest and ultimate annoyance to human survival. Sin is not only present in distant desert and jungle habitations, it is also very present in local towns and hamlets and more specifically, it is significantly present in the life and heart of every individual. *"For all have sinned and come short of the glory of God."*[71] The apparent inexhaustible record of crimes committed on this earth is a fulfilment of the prediction that *"evil men and seducers shall wax worse and worse"* (Rom 3:23). The presence and impact of sin is not reduced by the levy of government legislations or the issue of psychoanalytical prescriptions. The reduction of sin is only possible by the active power of the Holy Spirit at work in the life of an individual. Remission of sins literally means reduction, decrease or retardation thereof.

Reduction of sin in one's life is the objective operational target for daily living. Reduction or diminution of sin is not possible by mere human strategy and will power It demands the power of the Holy Spirit to actively battle and defeat the contributing forces that impact upon an individual. Reduction of sins is possible; hence John the Baptist preached repentance and baptism for the remission of sins. A threefold collection of spiritual agencies are at work for the benefit for each individual. Using the analogy of the train; In order to benefit from the reduction of sins on the way to the terminus, the passenger must first get on board the train. John preached a message of repentance.

Repent is an English word that derives from a Greek word "*metanoia*" literally meaning to turn around. Repentance is the act of turning around by expressing sorrow or regret for the thoughts conjured or actions taken. The act of repentance involves being turned in the right direction that leads to the progressive reduction of sin in one's life. Henceforth, Saul of Tarsus was travelling on the road to Damascus for the purpose of annihilating any new Jewish converts to Christianity. He was a learned and devout Jew of the tribe of Benjamin, and a prominent member of the Sanhedrin Council. Nevertheless, he was travelling on the wrong spiritual train. He needed to repent, change train and board the correct spiritual train that would result in the diminution and reduction of sin in his life. Despite the height of his scholasticism, he was woefully ignorant of his need to change direction. He needed a change agent and this was provided by Jesus Himself on the road to Damascus. Saul's train was derailed by the obstacle of Jesus' divine light that impacted the ground where he travelled and the thunderous voice sent him tumbling and helpless.

Upon recovery after being assisted to the point of rehabilitation, he was compelled to board another spiritual train, for which he needed a new ticket, the ticket of baptism. The contributing role played by Ananias in Saul's recovery was a result of direct instruction from Jesus. The same role is repeated by anyone who assists another in receiving a clear understanding of the purpose of the word of God.

Ananias declared that his role in assisting Saul was in order that he could regain his sight and be filled with the Holy Ghost.

Spiritual sight and the presence of the Holy Spirit are like Siamese twins, they are spiritually attached, and if separated, the Holy Spirit will endure but spiritual sight will diminish to a terminal end. Saul, without the presence of the Holy Spirit was spiritually blind. The impact of his temporary optical blindness was a catalyst that impacted his knowledge and hastened his spiritual anointing. The combination of his academic qualifications coupled with the zeal with which he pursued his task of retribution, enabled him to be fast –tracked into the new conversion process. In three days he was transformed from being Saul the persecutor to Paul, the baptized Apostle of Jesus Christ. He heard the message of the gospel from direct source, believed its messenger and responded with an immediate decision to be baptized.

What is Baptism?

Baptism is a public demonstration of an expression of internal spiritual conversion. It is a formal spiritual ceremony that demonstrates an individual being literally and totally immersed in water and the agent pronouncing baptism in the name of the Father, the Son, and the Holy Spirit.

The introduction of baptism to the Christian Church was heralded by the ministry of John the Baptist. John was not christened with the name Baptist, but was named under specific instruction from an angel to his father Zacharias. *"Thou shalt call his name John"* (Lk 1:13). John, cousin of Jesus, was the forerunner who paved the way for the arrival of Jesus on the Jerusalem circuit. His was ministry featured an uncompromising message that demanded repentance followed by baptism. John's boldness was highlighted by his temerity, to call the Pharisees and Sadducees, to their faces, a *"generation of vipers"* (Matt 3:7).

They came, with astonishment, to see for themselves the remarkable display of spiritual converts being immersed in the Jordan river. There is no record that confirms any significant conversion from the ranks of the Pharisees or Sadducees. John, however, preached that a person without repentance and baptism is as a fruit tree that bore no fruits and was liable for the consequence of being cut down and cast into a fire. Baptism therefore became the new rite that placed the new converts on the right spiritual road.

Inasmuch as John baptized with water, he declared in reference to Jesus, that there was one coming after him who was mightier that he and would baptize with the Holy Ghost and with fire (Matt 3:11). This new method of spiritual induction was not understood by all, yet it is evident that many, by faith, accepted the message of repentance and were baptized by John. This decision represented their decision to enter the Christian race. To the surprise of John, one significant candidate approached him with a request for baptism. Jesus, the One whom John had prophesied was coming to baptize with fire and the Holy Ghost, came and requested to be baptized by John.

There was, undoubtedly, a surprise reaction on John's face because baptism was the projected requirement for sinners and Jesus was understood to be the One whose life was without sin. The inference of Jesus' request was that he was not entirely sinless and was therefore in need of baptism. The doubt that arose was quickly dispelled when Jesus stated; *"suffer it to be so now: for thus it becometh us to fulfil all righteousness"* (Matt 3:15). If there arose any element of doubt, before or after, this act of Jesus and the subsequent response that followed has solidified the need and method for baptism.

The need for baptism is accentuated by the fact that every human individual is born into a family of sinners. *"For all have sinned and come short of the glory of God"* (Rom 3:23). The birth of Jesus was not the conclusion of Mary's impregnation by man, it was, said an angel; *"that which is conceived in her is of the Holy Ghost"* (Matt 1:20). Hence, Jesus was conceived of divine seed and was delivered into this world though the immaculate birth passage of a human surrogate. His flawless life and conclusive acceptance by His Father has bolstered the method and power of this spiritual enabling catalyst. Human beings are not born of the blood of heavenly royalty, however, through the rite of baptism, rebirth and spiritual regeneration, they are automatically ascribed family membership and full induction into the royal family of God is possible when the race is completed.

No one is exempt from the commitment thereof. Nicodemus, a ruler of the Jews, approached Jesus under the cover of darkness with an innocuous statement, and was greeted with an answer totally unrelated to the context of his approach. That is the remarkable role of the Holy Spirit. It is within the scope of our mental capacity to choose a pathway of extreme wickedness or to take an intelligent approach to the gospel. However, the Holy

Spirit will always endeavour to redirect our thinking and place us on a mental collision with the Lord. Jesus immediately directed his conversation to a higher sphere of knowledge. Jesus said to him; *"Except a man be born again, he cannot see the kingdom of God"* (Jn 3:3). This statement automatically led him to assume that Jesus was speaking about the possibility of literal rebirth. Jesus proceeded to clarify the meaning of his statement by saying; *"Except a man be born of water and of the Spirit of God, he cannot enter into the kingdom of God"* (Jn 3:5). Thus there are two necessary agents of saturation, the natural and the spiritual, water and the Holy Spirit.

The use of water is both significant as a cleansing agent and as an agent of spiritual regeneration. Water is a universal cleansing agent. Its significance in baptism is that it symbolises the outer cleansing of the individual who publically confesses their faith in God and acceptance of Jesus Christ as their personal saviour. No element of the outer body must be left above the immersion line of the water. The pursuance of a sinful life is in direct opposition to the life of a Christian. The pursuance of a sinful life is a blatant declaration of spiritual non-commitment. When an individual is convicted to live a new life as a follower of Jesus Christ, that decision must be confirmed and evident via an act of public declaration, it cannot be private or hidden from the view of the general public. To be engaged in a private baptism where spectators are prohibited is to express a sentiment of embarrassment about the stand that is being taken.

The cost of emancipation from sin was secured at the greatest expense that heaven could afford. Jesus, the Son of God, relinquished His throne at the right hand of His Father and ventured into this sin infested world in order that mankind may regain their place in the heavenly realm. Due to the significance of the cost, Jesus said; *"Whosoever therefore shall be ashamed of me and of my words in this adulterous and sinful generation; of him also shall the Son of man be ashamed, when he cometh in the glory of his Father with the holy angels"* (Mk 8:38). Jesus took our shame in order that we may adorn His glory. *"He was wounded for our transgressions; he was bruised for our iniquities"* (Isa 53:5). Jesus paid the ultimate price for our salvation with his life. He died that we might live eternally. His death was sufficient to prevent the eternal death of every individual.

As His death substituted for the death of every individual that has ever lived, so His burial represented the burial of the sin of every individual that has ever expressed their commitment to live a life in harmony with His wishes. *"Therefore we are buried with Him by baptism into death, that like as Christ was raised from the dead by the glory of the Father, even so we also should walk in the newness of life"* (Rom 6:4). As the earth facilitates the process of mortal decay and provides a barrier against the offensive odour thereof, likewise does baptism celebrate the death of the sinner and automatically induct the new righteous into the hall of fame of the righteous- free from the odour and the post-mortem rigidity of sin. The significance of burial is that: As with the burial of the dead, no element of the body is left to protrude above the surface of the earth. Baptism is not complete until every part of the body is submerged beneath the water line. Biblical baptism is not effected until and unless this process takes place.

At the moment of immersion and pronouncement, the sins of the candidate are spiritually crucified and buried with Jesus. Sin automatically loses its power to eternally destroy the human body. Baptism automatically launches the new member of heaven's family into the waiting room of those who will be transformed, body and soul, and will receive a new body "*like unto Jesus' glorious body*" (Pr 3:21). Baptism is therefore a psychological emancipating agent, liberating the old sinner from the stigma of sin, the servitude of sin, and the label of sinner. As soon as an individual is baptized he or she is automatically rechristened from the name "sinner" to the new name "*saint.*"

Thus, baptism is a conscious act and decision. It is not vicarious or by proxy. It is a decision that reflects the conscious understanding of one who has been taught, hence baby or infant baptism is not a confirmation of a conscious spiritual decision.

Baptism does not automatically preclude the new saint from the possibility of sinning, but it confers the individual with Holy Spirit assistance to continue the process of remission. After immersion the sinner is raised from beneath the water to live a new life in Christ in the likeness of His resurrection. Salvation and the reduction of sins (remission) is a progressive process. As a life guard rescues a drowning person from liquid fatality, the person being rescued is not saved when the pair reaches the shore. As long as the person being rescued cooperates with the competent life guard that person is saved on the way to the shore. When a baptized individual continues to walk in the life of Jesus, their experience does not wither and wane, rather; *"the path of the just is as the shining light, that shineth more and more unto the perfect day"* (Pr 4:18). Baptism is therefore only the start of brighter and better days for the Christian. Like Paul, the process commences when you join the Christian race.

The role of the Holy Spirit in the baptismal process is pivotal to the entire life of the newly baptised. To be baptized by the Holy Spirit is to invite the invisible power of God to saturate every fibre of the inner and outer body. The mortal life of an individual is a life, nevertheless, that is dead to spiritual regeneration. (Tim 5:6) Regeneration is initiated by the combined activity of the Godhead. God the Father *"showed His love for us while we were still sinners – His natural enemies – by giving His Son to die for us"* (Rom 5:8CW). The Holy Spirit acts upon the conscience by directing conscience pricking messages to the brain. The Holy Spirit is known as a quickening agent.

Those who live in the natural world live in response to the promptings of the prince of this world and thus are spiritually dead, existing in transgression and sins (Eph 2:1,2). Through the power of the Holy Spirit, the grace of God acts upon the conscience of individuals by activating and enabling the capacity of the mind to exercise a resentment for sin and to have a desire for spiritual growth. The Holy Spirit supplies the will power to resist unspiritual forces (Phil 2:13). That supply of power is not always supplied with dramatic force of wind or fire. The Spirit, more often than not, speaks with a still small voice (I Kg 19:12).

The Holy Spirit was present at the baptism of Jesus (Matt 2:16) and was pivotal to the strength that was required by Jesus to overcome the temptations of the Devil immediately thereafter. It is evident that the Holy Spirit was present and active at creation (Gen 1:2) and that He will remain active when this earth ceases to be (Rev 22:17). Before departing to reunite with His Father after His resurrection, Jesus told His disciples that He would leave them another Comforter. *"But the Comforter, which is the Holy Ghost, whom the Father will send in my name, He shall teach you all things and bring all things to your remembrance, whatsoever I have said unto you"* (Jn 14:26).

Whilst it is evident that the presence of the Holy Spirit after the ascension of Jesus was not an original appearance, Jesus was highlighting the commencement of a special dispensation. The baptism of the Holy Spirit as revealed by John and Jesus highlighted the activation of an internal saturation process that included the growth of spiritual understanding through learning, and a conscious control of the use of the entire body. The mind of sinful man is devoid of spiritual understanding, therefore spiritual lessons are necessary. *"The natural man receiveth not the things of the Spirit of God: for they are foolishness unto him, neither can he know them because they are spiritually discerned"* (I Cor 2:14).

The highlighted role of the Holy Spirit in the New Testament is the facilitation and the impartation of knowledge and understanding. The nature and attributes of the Godhead are particularly evident in the Holy Spirit.

- God is Eternal, He is without beginning and without end.[1]
- God is Omnipresent, He is everywhere.[2]
- God is Omniscient, He is perfect in knowledge.[3]
  God is Omnipotent, He is able to accomplish all that He wills.[4]
- God is Immutable; He is unchangeable.[5]

Whilst the personal presence of Jesus and the Father are currently exclusive to their residence in the heavenly realm, the Holy Spirit is the person from the Godhead that maintains a personal invisible presence instantly, everywhere. Thus Jesus bequeathed to His disciples the greatest atomic force that can be despatched to mankind without the possibility for immediate self-destruction. The Holy Spirit is not self-serving; His purpose is to lead the human mind, through the process of knowledge and understanding, to an experience that fully acquaints the individual with Jesus Christ. It may be that in the process of learning and understanding that a person becomes overwhelmed with ecstasy, but ecstasy is not the beginning of learning, it is a by-product.

The decision that launches an individual from being an ordinary spectator to be an Olympic Christian introduces an individual to an arena of dynamic possibilities. The Holy Spirit stands ready to despatch His power in order to assist any individual In their quest to achieve and excel in any sphere of human interaction. There are diversities of gifts that correspond to diversities of operations that are available to any individual. Prior to the introduction and study of Management Information Systems, the Holy Spirit was the genius at work organizing every sector of the earth's operations in the sky, on land and in water.

The capacity of man to study and harness any aspect of the earth's minuscule atoms, is possible because of the gifts that are imparted by the Holy Spirit. These gifts are not merely for spiritual operations, *"the manifestation of the Spirit is given to every man to profit withal"* (I Cor 12:7). The gift of coordination, the gift of beauty, the gift of invention, the gift of design, and the gift of management are all hallmark features of the operation of the Holy Spirit. As in the opening moments of creation, the Holy Spirit makes Himself available to anyone who has a desire to transform chaos into harmony. Thus, the decision to become a Christian Olympian is not confined to the narrow scope of praise and worship exercises. It is far more than declarations of praise, such as *"praise the Lord,"* or *"hallelujah."* Indeed, these are not the highest element of praise.

The greatest response that any individual can attribute to the glory of the Holy Spirit is to become a Christian Olympian through baptism and offer their entire cooperation to the spiritual makeover that will proceed thereafter. It is in the realm of the Spirit to perform miraculous feats on behalf of any individual. However, the reality is that the Spirit seeks man's cooperation in the development of man's natural abilities to their maximum human potential. Human beings are not gifted with wings as angels are, however, the Holy Spirit offers mankind the skill to invent and perfect flying crafts that leverage the possibility of human elevation even to the place where they are able to reach moons and stars.

The overall objective of the baptism of the Holy Spirit is to enable mankind to take the ultimate journey beyond the earth's atmosphere. The place that we know as heaven is beyond the reach and focus of man's optical and telescopic vision. Nevertheless, the Holy Spirit is the person in the Godhead that is working to secure a seat in that passage for everyone who will cooperate with him. Ultimately, when the sum of man's human transactions on this earth have been completed; it is the Holy Spirit who enables the transfer of passage for each qualified human passenger from this earth to the heaven that we aspire. Therefore, *"don't grieve the Holy Spirit who put His seal of approval on you when you gave your heart to Christ"* (Eph 4:30CW). The Spirit places His seal upon an individual's decision to become a Christian Olympian, He seals the quality and sincerity of human performance and after He has purged from man the thoughts and behaviour that are unlike God, He substitutes the righteousness of God that completes the surety of eternal salvation. Hence, *"grieve not the Holy Spirit of God, whereby ye are sealed unto the day of redemption"* (Eph 4:30).

The Holy Spirit places His seal upon the foreheads of mankind (Ezek 9:4; Rev 7:3). The forehead represents the progressive and ultimate mind-set of an individual. There are millions who desire to enter heaven's gates, but that desire is not at the forefront of their thinking or the response of their daily behaviour. There will be a sealing of minds that reflect and confirm the crest of man's spiritual intentions. The declaration of that sealing is projected thus; *"He that is unjust, let him be unjust still: and he which is filthy, let him be filthy still: and he that is righteous, let him be righteous still: and he that is holy, let him be holy still. And behold I come quickly; and my reward is with me, to give to every man according as his work shall be"* (Rev 22:11,12).

To be baptised by the Holy Spirit is to accept the invitation to allow the pattern and direction of your life to be prescripted by the invisible third person of the Godhead. His will and desire is to enable everyone who enters the Christian race to realise their successful completion. It is the desire of the Holy Spirit, who labours on behalf of the name and person of Jesus Christ, to report a full fruit of compliments from the successful achievements of the Christian Olympians. Paul, our fellow Olympian has commended all unto the only One who is able to guarantee success. *"Now unto Him that is able to keep you from falling, and to present you faultless before the presence of His glory with exceeding joy. To the only wise God our Saviour, be glory and majesty, dominion and power, both now and ever. Amen"* (Jude 24,25).

Notes

1. T.H.Jemison, <u>Christian Beliefs: Fundamental Biblical Teachings for Seventh-day Adventist College Classes</u>. Pacific Press Publishing Association: p:75
2. Ibid. p:75
3. Ibid. p:75
4. Ibid. p:75
5. Ibid. p:75

3 THE STRUGGLE AND THE FIGHT

The language of love that emanates from the Bible and the vocabulary of converted Christians have been misunderstood by many to assume that the daily lifestyle of a Christian is without struggle and conflict. Such belief could not be farther from the truth. Whilst love and harmony are the primary objectives of the Christian lifestyle, there appears to be an oppositional force that is in conflict with the will to be harmonious. The expressed declaration that *"God so loved the world that He gave His only Son to come here and die, that whosoever believes in Him will not perish but have eternal life"* (Jn 3:16CW); is consistent with the plea; *"Dear friends, let us love one another as God loves us"* (I Jn 4:7). Love and harmony are indeed primary objectives. However, individuals must be aware of oppositional forces that seek to thrash the hopes of anyone who aspires to be a Christian Olympian.

The roots of the conflict that has engulfed the world are found, ironically, in that very place where every Christian Olympian is destined to go. Here is the stark declaration of which everyone must be aware and understand; *"there was war in heaven"* (Rev 12:7). A controversy between God and Lucifer began in heaven. God's Son, Michael, (Whom we later know as Jesus when He became incarnate) and His loyal angels fought against Lucifer (whom we also know as Satan and the Dragon) and angels that were loyal to him. The details of the conflict are not recorded in Scripture, nevertheless, the inclusion of the name Dragon, implies that there was a fierce, blistering, cosmic battle that resulted in the defeat of the Dragon and his angels. The losers in the conflict were eternally banished from the place and presence of heaven. The sad news is that the Bible specifically states that they were cast out into the earth (Rev1:9).

Whether or not humans express belief in such concepts as devils and devil's angels, one thing is certain, that there is conflict on this earth that is sinister, manipulative and unfathomable. The inhabitants of this earth appear to be constantly at war. Death, discomfort and disharmony have been constantly increasing prevailing forces throughout the last century. The Dragon that was cast to the earth is also described as an accuser a persecutor and a destroyer. He and his angels oppose the decision of anyone who aspires or commit themselves to the lofty ambition of reaching that place from where they were banished. The devil and his angelic forces are vehemently opposed to Christian Olympians.

The statement; *"neither was their place found any more in heaven"* (Rev 12:8), declares that they can never return. Herein resides the foundational reason for human conflict, ecological and meteorological disasters on this earth. The misfortunes of those former cosmic residents, who have lost their place in the realms of eternity, have resulted in perpetual vindictiveness towards those who have the opportunity to aspire and reach that place where they can never return. Plainly speaking, their actions declare that if they cannot return to heaven, they intend to make it impossible for anyone to acquire the privilege which they have lost. Thus, there is constant conflict every day in the world and in the presence of anyone who aspires to be a Christian Olympian.

The prevailing struggle is evident in the resultant causes of discomfort, despair, despondency, disharmony, disaster, disease and death. The havoc that is wreaked by terrorists can be regarded as a segment of the strategy that has been unleashed upon the inhabitants of earth. Despite the evidence to suggest that the resources of this earth are sufficient for all of its inhabitants, there is a prevailing presence of inequity in every part of the globe. Whilst certain perpetrators are undeniably identifiable, the real culprits are invisible to the naked eye. *"For we wrestle not against flesh and blood, but against principalities and powers, against the rulers of the darkness of this world, against spiritual wickedness in high places"* (Eph 6:12). Having been converted to the new faith of Christianity, and having laid down the weapons that were integral to his position as a combatant for the Pharisees, Paul declared himself to be in the midst of another struggle.

The Christian Olympian must not be naïve to the forces of opposition that lurk along the pathway to destiny. The uses of the words strive, fight, and wrestle, highlight the need to be aware of forces of opposition at work against Christians to prevent their successful completion of the race. The use of these words as they are applied to the Christians' combat, are nevertheless, prescribed to behaviour that highlight battle, competition, struggle and grapple, the use of which prohibits mortal wounding or the intent thereof. Throughout centuries the enemies of Christians have been armed with carnal weapons, nevertheless, Christians are prohibited from the use of weapons for the purpose of inflicting mortal damage.

The Christians' fight entail their engagement against forces, seen and unseen, that obstruct and impede spiritual progress. The fight experience may be more appropriately described as a spiritual contest to overcome physical and psychological oppositional forces. The word fight, nevertheless, highlight the fact that oppositional forces do indeed inflict punitive and mortal damage, the likes of which can only be avoided or combated by determined and strategic retaliation.

It is both humiliating and demoralising to witness any form of physical or psychological bombardment upon a person who lacks the ability to retaliate or defend him or herself. Given that a decision to become a Christian Olympian is a decision that will, inadvertently, lead to experiences of spiritual opposition, the Christian Olympian, whilst naïve to the forces of opposition, must be aware that there is a source of spiritual amory at his or her disposal. Whilst the weapons available to the Christian are not carnal in nature, they are indeed colossal and powerful.

The battle that David experience when confronted with the gigantic stature of Goliath, is in part, instructive to the Christian who will be engaged in modern Christian warfare. The victory of a young boy who lacked military training and experience, was reckoned to be impossible over and against the formidable size and experience of the giant Goliath. Whilst the majority of spectators expressed pessimism for his victory, David embraced confidence in one insurmountable weapon, namely, the name of the Lord. David's reply to the arrogance, presumption, and dismissiveness of Goliath was: *"You've come to fight me with a sword, a spear and a javelin, but I come to you in the name of the Lord of hosts, the mighty God of Israel"* (I Sam 17:14). Thus David chose the ultimate weapon with which to arm himself in his impossible moment of combat. The Christian Olympian must find refuge and confidence in the name of the same God. *"The name of the Lord is a strong tower, the righteous runneth into it, and is safe"* (Prov 18:10).

A Tower of Strength

The first mention of the name of God is recorded in the very first line of the first book of the Bible. *"In the beginning God"* (Gen 1:1). The name of God that is recorded in the book of Genesis is *"Elohim."* Other names attributed to God throughout the Bible are Jehovah, El-Shaddai, El-Elyon, El-Olam and

Jehovah Sabaoth. Each name of God is given with a purpose that describes a distinct virtue or character of His nature in relation to a certain situation or person. These names demonstrate that no one name can adequately express His fullness. These give reflections of who He is, each name demonstrating a special virtue which other names bring out separately. Thus, God who is love, power and wisdom is also maker, judge and saviour to all.

The name Elohim describes the one and only true God who is Creator and Sustainer. When the planet was shrouded in chaos and darkness, it was Elohim who brought light, order and life. The process by which Elohim vocally called the systems of earth and the world into existence is known as divine fiat. Fiat translated means *"order or command."* Thus, on the first day Elohim said *"Let there be light"* (Gen 1:3). On the second day Elohim said *"Let there be a firmament in the midst of the waters"* (Gen 1:6). On the third day Elohim said *"Let the waters under the heaven be gathered together in one place, and let the dry land appear"* (Gen 1:9). On the fourth day Elohim said *"Let there be lights in the firmament of the heaven to divide the day from the night, and let them be for signs, and for seasons, and for days and years"* (Gen 1:14).

On the fourth day Elohim also *"made two great lights, the greater to rule the day and the lesser to rule the night. He made the stars also"* (Gen 1:16). On the fifth day Elohim said, *"Let the waters bring forth abundantly the moving creatures that hath life, and fowl that may fly above the earth in the open firmament of heaven*" (Gen 1:20). On the sixth day Elohim said, "*Let the earth bring forth the living creature after his kind, cattle and creeping thing*" (Gen 1:24). The pattern of creation reveals that Elohim's creation on each specific day made it possible for the succeeding day's creation to be sustained. Thus the creation of the second day was made sustainable because of the creation of the first day. More importantly, the creation of the sixth day was sustainable because of the creation of the previous five days. The crowning act of Elohim's creation came on the sixth day when Elohim said, "*Let us make man in our own image, after our likeness*" (Gen 1:26). On the seventh day Elohim "*ended his work which he had made, and he rested on the seventh day*" (Gen 2:3). Elohim "*blessed the seventh day and sanctified it*" (Gen 2:3).

The relevant lesson that is conveyed from the completion of the creation experience is that Elohim is able to create order beauty and intelligence from chaos and nothingness. The intelligence and genius of God in creation is applied to the practical needs of humanity. God did not create man and woman until there was adequate provision for their survival on earth. There is a large gap between understanding and accepting the genius of creation in contrast to understanding the devastation and disorder of sin.

The reality and impact of sin is a result of the unfettered choice of humanity. Adam and Eve chose to eat of the tree which God had forbidden. The result of that simple misguided choice has magnified into dynamic and disastrous proportions. Sin became injected into every organism that exists on the planet earth. The sponsor and escalator of sin is none other than the devil himself. One apparently simple wrong choice can bring disorder and disharmony to any cohesive system that Elohim has created for mankind.

When an individual makes the decision to join the Christian race and become a Christian Olympian, he or she is making a decision to place him or herself into the creative hands of Elohim. Whilst the devil is the chief sponsor for sin, sin itself could not have infiltrated the domain of humanity if Adam and Eve had remained loyal and obedient to the instructions of their creator. The decision to become a Christian Olympian is a decision that enables the Olympian to embark upon a path that leads back to the original state of man's previous sinlessness.

The presence of sin in our human environment is an epidemic that has generated behavioural personalities that are adverse to Elohim's prescribed edenic models. Whereas Elohim created beings that were harmonious in their behaviour, humanity today reflects diverse personalities that are foolish, disobedient, deceptive, lustful, envious and hateful in nature.

Psychologists and like professionals are not capable of analysing the behavioural deficiencies of every human being. Elohim, however, is sufficient for both the analytical needs and the transformational operation that will render any individual free from all psychoanalytical deficiencies. The Lord is a repairer of the breach that sin has inflicted upon the human person and personality. Sin may rob an individual of his or her confidence or humility to seek divine assistance, but the Lord is able to respond to the faintest cry of one who calls upon his name.

It was in the name of this God that David relied upon when he faced, what others considered to be an insurmountable challenge of Goliath. God did not fail him, and the towering figure of Goliath fell in defeat. Later in the tragic moments of his ethical failures with Uriah and Bathsheba, David expressed contrition of heart when he pleaded with God to have mercy upon him, wash and purge him thoroughly from his sin, and create a clean heart within him (Ps 51: 1,2,7,10). There is nothing that God cannot do for the sinner who calls upon His name. He is indeed a tower of strength for those who are engaged in spiritual combat, but He is equally a tower of strength to those who lose their moral spiritual balance. Christian Olympians must not fear in calling on Elohim for help and deliverance from any snare.

The Model of Justice

The strength and creativity of God is matched by His love and His justice. The name Jehovah supplements the name Elohim. Thus God is represented in the second and third chapter of the book of Genesis as *"Lord God."* A more precise interpretation of the Hebrew text declares the name Jehovah to mean *"the ever being."*1 This statement was indeed expressed to Moses when he sought for an answer to reply to those Egyptians who would desire to know the name of God. Jehovah's answer to Moses was; *"I AM WHO I AM."*[2] It is not possible to define or describe all that God is but the name Jehovah is given to us in order to express the substance of God's being.

Whilst the name Elohim assists in our understanding of a creative God who injected His personal breath into a lifeless man in order to cause life to commence in man, the name Jehovah is instructive in our understanding of His righteousness and His justice. The name Jehovah introduces us to a God who embraces standards. It is in the name Jehovah that we become aware of the *"Thou shalt"* and *"Thou shalt not's."* *"Of every tree of the garden thou mayest freely eat: But of the tree of knowledge of good and evil, thou shalt not eat of it: for in the day that thou eatest thereof thou shalt surely die"* (Gen 2:16). Humanity today is gifted with the vision of hind sight that allows us to recognize the freedom of volition that was been given to man.

The choice to eat or not to eat was an absolute privilege that was given to our predecessors in the Garden of Eden. However, the opportunity to experience the impact of disobeying the will of Jehovah was equally absolute. In as much as Elohim said, *"Let us make man in our image, after our likeness"* (Gen 1:26), the Lord God (Jehovah) demonstrated the standard of His righteousness when he excluded the pair that He had made in His image from the garden. *"Therefore the Lord God sent him form the garden. So He drove out the man; and He placed at the east of the garden of Eden Cherubims, and a flaming sword which turneth every way, to keep the way of the tree of life"* (Gen 3:23). It is instructive to note that from the very outset of man's creation, Jehovah established boundaries of His righteousness that was not permitted to be breached by someone whom he dearly loved.

The names of God are a transcript of His character. Mankind may not be capable of grasping a total understanding of the nature of God from one initial glance; however, progressive understanding is a secondary provision that is equally available. Whilst Elohim is the name by which He revealed Himself to Abraham, Isaac and Jacob, God declared to Moses; *"but by my name Jehovah was I not known to them"* (Ex 6:3). Thus God unfolded an aspect of Himself to Moses that was previously unrevealed to the early patriarch.

God cannot change for the better or for worse. He can never be greater or more holy than He is, nor can He be less so. Jehovah was not adding a new attribute; He was simply creating a greater revelation of what was already there. Jehovah is immutable, He is unchangeable, and He is perfect. He can never be greater or more holy than He is, nor can He be less so."[3] *"I am the Lord, I change not"* (Mal 3:6).

The attributes of God are absolute.

- God is Holy,[4] He is righteous,[5]
- He is just,[6] He is merciful,[7]
- He is full of loving-kindness,[8]
- He is gracious,[9] He is truth,[10]
- He is pure,[11] and
- He is love.[12]

No such person has been born among humanity except Jesus. Only a God can possess such attributes and equally possess the ability to activate all of them on behalf of humanity. The declarations of God's divine attributes may seem contradictory. However the birth, life and death of Jesus satisfies the answer to all questions. In Exodus 34:7 God declared Himself to be merciful and forgiving, yet He also declared that He would *"by no means clear the guilty"* (Ex 34:7). There is a penalty for spiritual disobedience, however, the storehouse of Jesus' largess is substantial enough to compensate for every violation.

Sinners who are convicted by the Holy Spirit of moral violations, and accept their conviction, are absolved from guilt due to the capacity of Jesus to assume guilt on their behalf and accept their penalty. Thus the penalty for sin is satisfied and the sinner's guilt is liquidated because Jesus becomes the substitute sinner in order to satisfy the need for reparation. It is, on one hand complex, due to the myriad violations of man's morality, yet, on the other hand it is amazingly simple, all because of Jesus' marvellous ability to satisfy the penalty for every violation. When the reality of His substitution is understood, that understanding should cause all Christian Olympians to express abundant gratitude and praise to the one who has done so much for them.

This gratitude was demonstrated in composite fashion when a woman, dragged and accused by a group of hypocritical Pharisees, was cast at the feet of Jesus accused of the violation of adultery. *"Moses told us that such a person should be stoned to death. What do you say"* (Jn 8:5CW)? The response of Jesus was a masterful demonstration of wisdom, mercy, justice, truth, love, and righteousness. The same law that they quoted stated that both the woman and the man should be stoned to death, but they, who stated that they had caught the woman in the very act of adultery, brought the woman in absence of the man. There was an obvious imbalance in their standard of justice.

Jesus, who is the standard for Justice, could not negate their accusation; however, neither could He give an answer that would, by proxy, justify the guilty. He had to satisfy the standard that was required of the name Jehovah. One simple answer to the accusers and the accused satisfied the requirements of all of His attributes. To the accusers He said; *"He that is without sin among you, let him cast a stone at her"* (Jn 8:7). When in shame and self-condemnation they had all departed from the scene, He said to the woman; *"Neither do I condemn thee, go and sin no more"* (Jn 8:11). With those words of wisdom, justice had been served, mercy and grace had been applied, loving-kindness had been administered, and holiness was offered in substitute for her sin. This is the miracle that is constantly repeated on behalf of every individual who enters the Christian race.

The lot of a Christian Olympian is a treasured position that mortal currency cannot afford. Every moment that a person discloses his or her desire to become a Christian Olympian, Jehovah matches their desire by making it possible for His righteousness to be transferred and replace their sinfulness. Like the woman caught in the act of adultery, Jehovah makes the application of His righteousness a practical application to the life of the sinner. Sin condemns, but He makes righteousness available to all. As the accusers were disarmed without the aid of carnal weapons, so by calling on the name of the Lord every sinner can avail himself or herself of the most powerful weapon that is available to mankind – The Name of God.

The Abundant Provider

The literal reading of the Hebrew text is translated: *"And it was*

Abram a son of ninety years and nine years, that Jehovah appeared to Abram and said to him, I am God the Almighty."[13] Whilst omnipotence is one of the listed attributes of God, ancient Hebrew text does not support the modern assertion that this third name of God refers to his immense might and awesome power. God is indeed a God of might and strength, but this third name describes a different understanding of the Almighty. God is almighty because of His power and ability to carry out the will of His divine nature. The God who is described by the name Jehovah can love and save, but He cannot do so at the expense of His integrity. The Hebrew name by which God introduces Himself to Abram is not Elohim or Jehovah. This name that God used in this context is the name El-Shaddai.

Whilst the word El is commonly recognized as the name for God, its' true interpretation derives from the Semitic name for deity which often appears in compounds with proper names.[14] Thus we have become acquainted with such familiar titles as El-ohim, El-Shaddai, El-Elyon and El-Olam. The name of God that introduces Him as El-Shaddai is the product of the combination of the words El and shaddai. The word shaddai derives from the root word "*shad*", meaning "*breast.*" The name Shaddai primarily refers to one who is breasted. Thus the composite name for God as introduced in Gen 17:1 is interpreted as "*the breasted one.*"

Whilst the deity of heaven is universally recognized as a

male or masculine deity, the name El- Shaddai appears to be attributing female attributes to one who is masculine. Correct understanding of the name El-Shaddai should not be perverted by modern connotations of breasts. Another interpretation of this ancient name is translated to mean "*mighty teats*."[15] The connotation that this organ of modern sexual eroticism implies a duality in divine sexuality is not the intent of the divine name. Its' obvious connection with the breasts of a woman should not lead the reader to leap to a conclusion of sexual connotations, but should lead instead to the provision of sustenance that a woman would supply to her offspring. El-Shaddai is therefore a provider whose mighty teats is able to supply in abundance to one and all who would follow Him.

The age of Abram and the twenty four year gap between his departure from Ur, lends itself to an understanding of the introduction of this additional name of the divine deity. When Abram departed from Ur at the age of seventy five, he departed under the assurance that God would fulfil His promise to bless him with abundance. "...*I will make thee a great nation, and I will bless thee, and make thy name great; and thou shalt be a blessing. And I will bless them that bless thee, and curse him that curseth thee, and in thee shall all families of the earth be blessed*" (Gen 12:3). Given that modern social scientists have revealed that moving house ranks in the top ten causes of stress, such as divorce and bereavement, we, by inference are led to understand the stress that was experienced by Abram, his family and the family of his nephew, Lot.

They gathered all of their substance. Whilst there are no reported statistics of the extent of their substance, the inference is that the addition of servants and livestock equates to a substantial group and possessions. Whilst the faith of seventy five year old Abram was significant, the faith of ninety nine year old Abram must have been threadbare in the absence of the fulfilment of the mighty promise. Hence at age ninety nine God appeared to bolster His original promise by the revelation of a name that offered greater assurance. "*I am the Almighty God.*" I am El-Shaddai. I am the breasted one. I am the one who has the abundance of milk and I am the one who is able to supply all of your needs. "*...Walk before me and be thou perfect. And I will make my covenant between me and thee, and I will multiply thee exceedingly*" (Gen 17:1,2).

The broader revelation of God's divine attributes that was conveyed in the introduction of this new name was intended to engender greater confidence in a God who requires substantial faith of those who aspire to benefit from His abundant outpouring of substance. The application of faith and the rewards thereof firmly secured Abraham's place in the halls of fame and faith. That legacy of one who stepped out in faith under the assurances of El-Shaddai is meant to be a model to demonstrate that all things are possible when an individual places his or her trust in the God who is able to provide in abundance. To one who is apprehensive about becoming a Christian Olympian, the use of this name and the call upon the God of this name is intended to dispel all doubts and apprehensions that would hinder from taking the leap of faith.

The challenge that is facing all potential Christian Olympians is the challenge to step out from their familiar environment and allow El-Shaddai to lead them into unchartered territory. There is a chasm between the spiritual philosophies of the world and the spiritual philosophy of God for His people. All who are to be identified as God's true people are to separate themselves from the environment and lifestyle of those who live contrary to the will of God. Abram was called to move out, in faith, from the polytheistic environment to an environment that sponsored the belief in one God. Modern Christians are called upon to remove themselves from the environment of anyone who walks and lives a disorderly lifestyle.

The challenge that was extended to Abram is the same challenge that is extended to every non-Christian; Walk! The challenge of one who would become an Olympic Christian is the challenge to walk away from the environment that will hinder spiritual growth. This is not merely to be a pedestrian, but to continue walking at a pace and direction of God's approval. Do not allow age, profession, family or possessions to hinder your leap of faith.

This movement of faith is synonymous to a grain of sand that irritates and agitates an oyster in anticipation of a great pearl. The anticipation and irritation is the outworking of a process that enables the walker to listen to the directions and instructions of an invisible God. This understanding is in contrast to following the steps of a visible and audible God. Thus, like Abraham, the Christian Olympian moves out from his or her familiar environment and walks the new unknown pathway to a life that will yield in abundance.

The assurance that continual walking and abundant rewards are possible resides in the assurance that is resident in the name El-Shaddai. The breasted one, the one who has mighty teats, is able to nourish and supply in multiple complexities. The assurance given to Abram has come from the God (Adonai) who has demonstrated His power to create something out of nothing, and from the God (Jehovah) who has given his oath of justice. Given that He had previously given His assurance that He would make Abram into a great nation, the introduction of the name El-Shaddai leads to the understanding that God is able to supply in abundance, even as Abram's descendants continue to multiply and become as numberless as the stars.. The seal of assurance was further demonstrated by the expansion and enhancement of Abram's name to Abraham.

The promise of the assurance of abundant provisions comes

with the command for continual compliance. El-Shaddai demanded of Abraham that he walk before Him and be perfect. The use of the word perfect infers that Abraham was expected to be flawless in his daily living. The demand to be perfect is not instant and absolute, it is progressive and cumulative. The promise of abundant provision from El-Shaddai – the breasted one, was given with the provision that Abraham continued to walk before God in a manner that was acceptable to God. Therefore, as long as Abraham did not stop his continual walk El-Shaddai would not cease His continual outpouring of abundant blessings.

The relevance of this promise to the modern Olympian resides in its extension to all of Abraham's descendants. The promise and assurance of abundant provisions is therefore not limited to the immediate Abrahamic family, (those whom we identify as of Jewish ancestry) but is extended to the many nations who embrace the command to walk before El-Shaddai. When a person becomes a Christian, he or she automatically becomes a follower of Jesus Christ. *"And if ye be Christ's, then are ye Abraham's seed, and heirs according to the promise"* (Gal 3:29).

There is no prohibition to the range of people who can embrace the possibilities that are available through El- Shaddai. All people from all nations can become an Olympic Christian. *"There is neither Jew nor Greek, there is neither bond nor free, there is neither male nor female: for ye are all one in Christ Jesus"* (Gal 3:28), and all are potential beneficiaries of the promise of abundance.

A Beloved Master

One of the noticeable moral deficiencies in the promotion of liberty in western societies is the promotion of promiscuity, which in turn sponsors a lack of deference toward dignitaries, and, more importantly, a lack of deference toward God. During His conversation to Abram in a vision, God introduced himself by yet another name which presents another aspect of His character in His relationship to mankind. In His vision to Abram He is presented as Lord God, literally, *"Adonai Jehovah."*[17] Modernist thinkers need to pay particular attention to the permanent endearing attributes that are portrayed in this name.

The Hebrew word *"Adon"* literally means *"Lord or Master."*[18] Adonai is the plural of the singular word Adon. This word specifically translates the meaning of God's lordship over and above His citizens. As Master Jehovah - God is sovereign, not because He is tyrannical, but because His lofty excellence is demonstrated in His ability to be, as Isaiah described, *"high and lifted up"* (Isa 6:1). The word *"Adon"* also conveys the relationship of a husband to his wife. The church of God has always been regarded as feminine in gender. Jeremiah records that God has likened the daughter of Zion to *"a comely and delicate woman..."* (Jer 6:2), and the apostle John records the words of an angel who referred to the redeemed of God as *"the bride, the lamb's wife…"* (Rev 21:19). Herein, we find that the use of this name of God commands attention and understanding of one is both commanding and endearing.

The Olympic Christian is called upon to recognize that there is no harshness or contradiction between the use and application of the name as it is applied to one person. Sin has ascribed and applied a negative connotation to role of a master to a servant. Adonai, on the other hand, is the God who is worthy of the praise of His angelic host and also sufficient for the needs of His human subjects. Adonai is the one who confirmed to Moses that He was the one who made the mouth of mankind. He is the one who promised to accompany and empower Joshua in the promised land. He is the one who empowered the ministries of Gideon, Samuel and Samson. By virtue of His name, Adonai is the one who has demonstrated that He is sufficient to fit and equip anyone for the work that He has committed to them.

Whereas we have thus far concentrated on the loftiness of God that is conveyed in the name Adonai, the other interpretation of His betrothal to a comely and delicate woman is equally important. The Olympic Christian must understand that his or her commitment to Adonai is not a relationship that is dominated and or abused by a master figure; rather it is one that is as a marital relationship. Adionai is not just Lord and master;

He is also a devoted husband to the one whom He loves.

The conception of being the spouse of God is intended to highlight the endearing relationship that Adonai seeks to develop with each individual who commits him or herself into His care. When an individual has not expressed any commitment to the cause and will of God, he or she is considered to be a child of the world. *"The World"* is a terminology that is generally referring to those who express a determined position that is contrary to the will and wishes of God. The people of the world do not know Adonai, therefore they act as they please. Those who are affiliated with Adonai are governed by principles that are reflective of a marital bond and relationship.

Adonai declares that He is married to those who commit themselves to Him. As a committed and faithful spouse, Adonai is grieved when His wife turns back and returns to the practices of the world. His relationship with His spouse, His church, is personal and intimate. In his letter to the church at Ephesus Paul admonished the husbands to love their wives *"as Christ Loved the church..."* (Eph 5:25). Adonai is is committed a committed spouse who has vowed to take care of all of the necessities of His wife. As a result of His dedication to provide, fortify and eventually save his spouse from a world of sin, Adonai will not allow His affection for His wife to contaminate and compromise His judgement and justice.

As husband and God, He is both lover and judge. It is perhaps possible that if the spouse of a judge was to be arraigned in court, that judge would remove himself from the position as a sitting judge in order to avoid the perception of a conflict of advocacy. Adonai, on the other hand is a God who cannot lie, and will not lie. He will not allow His devotion to be contaminated by His love. Therefore Adonai expresses His dismay and discontent with behaviour that is unbecoming of a faithful spouse. Adonai will not defend and justify His spouse if she engages in behaviour that is akin to a harlot, neither will He countenance the behaviour of a spouse who places a price tag on her acts of domestic or priestly duties.

The wife of Adonai will not receive any unfavourable and unjust favour from her husband, neither will she be neglected in the hour of final deliverance from this world.

Notes

1. Karl Feyerabend, Langenshedt's Pocket Hebrew Dictionary.
   Hodder and Stoughton. p:122.
2. The Interlinear Hebrew. Aramaic. Ex3:14. p:146.
3. Jemison, p:76
4. Ibid.
5. Ibid.
6. Ibid.
7. Ibid.
8. Ibid.
9. Ibid.
10. Ibid.
11. Ibid.
12. Ibid.
13. Jay P.Green, Sr, The Interlinear Bible.
    Hendrickson Publishers. Peabody. Massashusetts. Gen 17:1
14. William L.Holladay,
    A Concise Hebrew and Aramaic Lexicon of the Old Testament.
    William B.Eardmans Publishing Company. P:15.
15. Ibid.p: 361
16. Jane E. Lynthgoe, The Meaning of Al Shadi (El Shaddai) in Ancient Hebrew.
    April 28: 2008. Ieue.org/profiles/blogs/20096.36 BlogPost:5816
17. Norman Henry Snaith, The Hebrew Old Testament.
    The British and Foreign Bible Society. London.
18. Holladay. p:4

4 ON YOUR MARKS

Athletes and spectators around the world are familiar with the words that set competitors on their alert for the start of a race. The nervousness of the athletes and the thrilling expectation of the spectators combine to yield a scene of thrilling drama. In decades past, the critical eyes of the human monitors were the judges that determined whether or not there was a false start. Modern Olympiads are equipped with electronic monitors on the starting blocks. These electronic monitors are critical in detecting the slightest movement that would translate into a warning or disqualification. The second sound of the starter's pistol is gravely disappointing, both to the athlete and to the spectators because two false starts equate to automatic disqualification.

The starting of the Christian race is not so punitive. There is vast scope for the redemption of misbehaviour or misapplication at the start of or during the race. However, corrective behaviour must be applied in order to successfully complete the race. The latitude that is afforded a Christian Olympian is qualitative. Moreover the description given may appear to be quantitative, depending upon which bible version you read. The King James version declares; *"For a just man falleth seven times and riseth up again: but the wicked shall fall into mischief"* (Pr 24:16). The Clear Word, however, conveys greater scope for the latitude of

Christian error. "*No matter how often an honest man suffers calamity, he finds courage to rise again; but repeated disasters overcome the wicked*" (Pr 24:16CW).

The Christian Olympian must be aware of the myriads of pitfalls that can hamper his or her race, however, he or she must be equally aware that the grace of God offers available assistance in many forms that is encouraging and redeeming. For example, when we think of an Olympic race, the immediate consideration begs the question; how fast will the athletes run? The second consideration is; who will be the three front runners. In the Olympics, the focus is always predominately on the winner. However, in the Christian Olympics "*the race is not to the swift nor the battle to the strong...*" (Ecc 9:11). The ultimate objective of the Christian Olympian is to complete the race regardless of the position that he or she may finish.

The ultimate qualifying necessity of the Christian Olympian is not the position that he or she may finish, but it is the qualifying mark that they carry with them to the end of the race. When Jesus was nearing the completion of His race, He declared to His disciples, "*the prince of this word cometh, and hath nothing in me...*" (Jn 14:30). This was Jesus' declaration that He had not yielded to any of Satan's temptations. It was as a humble Lamb that Jesus succumbed to the ravages of sin and it was as a suffering servant that He fulfilled the requirements that were necessary for every man's salvation and reconciliation. Having suffered and died according to the requirements for human salvation, Jesus ensured His Father's approval by restraining the congratulatory spirit of Mary as He prohibited her from contaminating an excellent race.

Jesus' instructive words of restraint to Mary-*"Touch me not; for I am not yet ascended to my Father"* (Jn 20:17), are equally instructive words to every Olympian who desires to receive the medallion that utterly, eternally, emancipates from sin. Just as Jesus' ministry and sacrifice needed the ultimate endorsement of His Father, so does every Olympic Christian need the same mark of approval in order to enter a sinless eternity. That approval is both necessary and obtainable. Jesus longs to say to all who complete the Christian race; *"Come ye blessed of my Father, inherit the kingdom prepared for you from the foundation of the world"* (Matt 25:34). That ultimate accolade is only possible when the Father sees, in one who has been tainted by sin, the eradication of every jot, spot or wrinkle that resembles sin. Jesus is the only person that can guarantee that possibility and He is able to confirm that distinction by placing His seal upon the life of any repentant sinner.

The Seal of Jesus

The book of Revelation is unique among the books of the Bible due to the fact that it was specifically dictated to the last remaining apostle, from the days of Jesus' ministry, as a letter coming directly from Jesus. The apostle John was simply the penman for the messages that represent *"The Revelation of Jesus Christ..."* The book of Revelation predicts many graphic events that will take place before the end of the world. Amongst other disclosures, this last book of the Bible is unique for its graphic description of sequential apocalyptic events that will pre-empt the end of the world. After the record of Jesus' ascension in the book of Acts, there is no record of His whereabouts until John was permitted to see Him in His majestic and priestly garments and apply this recorded in the first chapter of the book of Revelation. One of the first records that John was instructed to write was a series of letters that was penned to seven Churches that were located in the provinces of Asia Minor.

The number seven is a recurring digit throughout this book.

- Seven letters are written to seven Churches.
- Seven angels administer seven seals.
- Seven trumpets herald the outpouring of seven plagues which in turn represent;
- Seven bowls of God's wrath.

The seven letters, seven Churches and seven seals each cover synchronized eras of time, each denoting progress and countdown to the end of the world. Whilst the seals represent the end of a specific era for a specific Church or group of people, the seventh seal highlights the administration of God's approval and endorsement upon the lives of the last group of people who are obedient and loyal in an era of blatant blasphemy and apostasy.

Today, Christian Olympians are living in the era of the Church that is covered by the letter to the churches that are in Laodicea. The Laodicean era of churches is the last of seven eras. Christians living in this era have been prophesied as demonstrating remarkable self-confidence and self-complacency without the spiritual substance to support their pretentions. Whilst the nations of the world are busy sauntering along and consumed with the intoxication of their own agenda, God is bringing down the curtain on the lasts acts of earth in order to commence the events of a new heaven and a new earth where there will be no sin. The commencement of a new era where sinless people dwell, demands implicit and explicit behaviour that qualify the new residents for occupancy in that land of bliss. The book of Revelation therefore highlights the fact that God is placing His mark, His seal, upon the lives of those who meet the measure of His righteous standard.

Countless tragedies on earth have provoked millions of people to question the love and sovereignty of God over the affairs of this earth. The events that are recorded in the first three verses of the seventh chapter of the book of Revelation highlight the fact that God is indeed in charge and that His angels are actively conducting His biddings. The words; "*after these things…,*" refer to the conclusion of events that have transpired over the eras of the seven churches. Having permitted mankind to exercise the scope of their morality Jesus Christ stands ready to bring an end to this great earthly drama.

The end would have already come had it not been for the fact that Jesus Christ extended magnanimous mercy to those who have not yet entered the Christian race. Angels are ministering servants who act upon God's instructions to intervene in the affairs of mankind. Four angels, denoting angels of strength, are positioned at the inhabitants of the earth from imminent and pressing disaster. Given that the earth is neither flat nor square, the four corners mentioned are literally the four directions of the compass; namely, north, south, east and west.

When the word "*wind*" is used in prophetic context, it generally refers to strife, commotion, or war (Jer 25:31-33. Jer 4;11-13. Zec 7:14). Four angels who are positioned at the four pivotal directions positions of earth are actively withholding the destructive forces that are pressing to be unleashed upon the hapless people of earth. In the past twenty years, this earth has experienced an inundation of destructive forces. Tsunamis, floods, earthquakes, famine, wars and terrorism have deluged, ravaged and battered this earth. The actions of the four angels highlight a message of pessimism which declares. Whatever disasters have gone prior to this day, greater and more catastrophic disasters are yet to come. Those disasters are even now pressing to be unleashed.

The message from the disposition of the four angels leads us to assume that they are tired of holding back the winds of strife, or that they are overly stressed due to the force that is amassing, or that they are demonstrating some eagerness to depart from their positions in order that the next phase of deliverance may take its course. If we would soberly consider the impact of the destructive forces that have passed, we would tremble to envisage the sheer catastrophe that is pressing to be released. The coming forces are so catastrophic that it takes the strength of mighty angels to restrain their impact.

Wrapped up within the restraint of the four angels and the message of the single angel who heralds a message from the east - is a message of salvation, grace and hope. God has trusted servants that are embedded amongst the multitude of people in the world. God is not willing that any should perish. Therefore, He has despatched one angel to deliver a message of hope and assurance. The message of hope simply translated is that God will seal and save His servants from the disaster that is to come. The expanded message leads to the understanding that those who will be saved are those who respond positively by free volition. Choice for God is a decision of free will. Those who firmly decide to serve the Lord with heart mind and soul will be candidates for the seal of God.

The seal of God represents God's system for approving the belief and behaviour of those who genuinely call upon His name. In as much as Jesus said, "*Not every one that saith unto me, Lord, Lord, shall enter the kingdom of heaven*" (Matt 7:21), Jesus will only commission the sealing of those who embrace an accurate and sincere belief of His teachings. The key concern for an Olympic Christian today is that his or her belief in God synchronizes with the word of God. The Bible declares that there is "*One Lord, one faith, one baptism, One God and Father*" (Eph 4:5,6), yet there are countless Christian denominations with varying beliefs. The acceptance of varying and contrasting beliefs would infer that God is sponsoring religious confusion. God is not a God of confusion but a God of unity, therefore, the application of His seal upon the foreheads of His worshippers would represent the greatest accolade that they can receive. The forehead represents the seat of one's intelligence. God is therefore highlighting the message that He is not sealing emotionalism but He is sealing intelligent spiritual commitment.

The seal of God represents God's system for accepting the worship of those who call upon His name. The application of worship is the outward and inward form of adoration that an individual attributes to a deity. The one and only true God who rules the universe will not accept any form of worship that violates His specific mandate. God gave a specific mandate to both Cain and Abel. Whilst Abel complied with the mandate, his brother Cain exercised innovativeness and individuality by bringing to God the best fruit that he had gathered from his crops. *"The Lord had respect unto Abel and his offering. But unto Cain and his offering He had not respect"* (Gen 4:4,5). God is consistent with His request for worship. False worship or disobedient worship will not meet God's approval.

Due to the fact that the seal of God reflects His acceptance of worship, it has been prophesied that the amount of people who desire to be sealed but, regrettably, will fall into the wrong category are *"many"* (Matt 7:22). Thousands of Christian denominations and millions of worshippers all desire to receive the approval of God. The tragedy of the devotion of many worshippers is that they are sincerely committing themselves to marvellous and commendable spiritual acts, in the name of Jesus. Yet, when He returns to gather His worshippers for eternity, He will disown their acts of devotion. Matthew talks of many prophets, many exorcists who engage and confront the forces of evil, and many philanthropists, who perform marvellous and commendable acts, yet lack some vital ingredient of character that Jesus is not willing to endorse.

On the day of His resurrection when Jesus declared to Mary, *"touch me not for I am not yet ascended to my Father..."* (Jn 20:17), He was declaring that His Father had to endorse the completion of His ministry. In as much as such high standard applied to the ministry of Jesus, the same standard is needed in order for the redeemed to gain access into heaven. Jesus' blood must cover and eradicate every spot or wrinkle of sin that affects every sinner, and His endorsement of their integrity must be able to attract the endorsement of His Father. Indeed, the Father must be able to say of all who would enter heaven; *"this is my beloved son, beloved daughter, in whom I am well pleased."*

When the children of Israel were preparing to depart from Egypt, their preparation demanded the presence of a distinctive mark upon the posts of their doors. *"And ye shall take a bunch of hyssop, and dip it in the blood that is in the basin, and strike the lintel and the two side posts with the blood that is in the basin; and none of you shall posts go out at the door of his house until the morning. For the Lord will pass through to smite the Egyptians; and when he seeth the blood upon the lintel, and on the two sides pasts, the Lord will pass over the door, and will not suffer the destroyer to come in unto your houses to smite you"* (Ex 12:22,23). In similar manner, the seal of God will be applied to the forehead of God's faithful servants.

The seal of God on the forehead will be a mark that is invisible to the human eye. The significance of the forehead is that it represents the seat of intelligence. Hence, God in not seeking to apply an outward mark, rather, He is seeking to endorse the level of intelligence, sincerity and integrity that exist within the heart of those who claim to be followers of Jesus Christ. The Olympic Christian, therefore, must not only bare the name of Jesus, he or she must also reflect the character of Jesus.

The Mark of the Beast

If the seal of God is the mark to which all should aspire, the mark of the beast is the blot that all should seek to avoid. The Laodicean era is the last of the seven churches to which John the Revelator was commissioned to write. It is in the final and closing scenes of this church that a great battle for spiritual supremacy and worship is ensued between the two great forces of the universe. The last remaining individuals on earth are being positioned to be engaged as soldiers in a cataclysmic conflict between God and Satan. The final stages of the great plan of salvation are being culminated with tremendous detail and emphasis. Jesus is preparing to fulfil the promise that He made to His disciples in John 14:1-3.

In anticipation of the greatest earthly coronation rally, spiritual forces are rallying and demonic forces are troubling. Political forces are crumbling and ecclesiastical forces are corralling. A dramatic spiritual showdown is being dramatized between God's agents of faith and Satan's agents of violence. Worshippers of obedience will demonstrate their opposition and rejection against a mark of spiritual defiance. As there was war in heaven prior to the ejection of Lucifer from the premises of heaven, likewise, there will be war on earth prior to the ejection and eradication of Satan from the face of the earth. The scope of the emerging war will be a beastly war with eternal consequences.

5   BEASTLY

When the word beast is ascribed to the behaviour of an individual it automatically conveys the understanding that a certain individual is animal-like in their behaviour. The ascription of the word beast to an organisation confers the same animal-like behaviour to that organisation.

The twelfth chapter of Revelation paints a picture of amazing contrasts. A woman and her child are being challenged by a beast with seven heads. Whist this appears to be a challenging portrayal of extreme proportions, the portrayal of the extremes is significant in conveying the enormous importance of the outcome of a pending battle. Lucifer, the salubrious, eminent and glamorous angel who once occupied a position next to the monarchs of heaven fell from his coveted position and adopted the likeness and behaviour of a beast. After he fell from his coveted position, the former covering cherub transformed his behaviour into the assimilation of a serpent that crawls, a barbarian, and a deceiver to the entire human race. The combinations of coveted attributes were now turned malignant thus earning him the new title of dragon.

The dragon fought against the monarchs of heaven and lost. His deceptive persuasiveness manipulated and beguiled one third of the heavenly host, thus ensuring him a vast army of fallen angels to attend his bidding. Whist guile and subterfuge have become the primary agents for his approach to mankind; his core objective is the comprehensive obstruction and blockage of salvation to all mankind. The dragon is opposed to the reunification of the citizens of earth with the kingdom of God. Despite all the wiles that may be conspired against him or her, when an individual becomes a Christian Olympian, he or she is blessed with the power to overcome and ultimately secure the winner's accolade.

Whilst Satan has been cast down and out from heaven, his powers of annihilation have been countered by the introduction of another contrasting allegorical creature. The dragon is being opposed by a Lamb. Theoretically, a lamb is no match for the torturous aggression of a dragon, however, when the lamb is the Lamb that takes away the sins of the world, the analysis of that Lamb's power has to be reassessed. Whilst Satan is the dragon, Jesus is the Lamb. The Christian Olympian may find himself or herself centred in the crucible of the heat of oppression day and night, but a loud voice of deliverance is heard from the depths of heaven. An heavenly herald has sent out a message of hope that counteracts the tortuous flames of the dragon's worst oppression.

At a time when deliverance seems implausible, a voice from heaven proclaims that salvation is within the grasp of every

Christian. Dramatic assurance is proclaimed by the heavenly herald declaring that power and strength from the heavenly kingdom is made available to the Christian Olympian. Whilst the dragon may breathe out its fire to consume the blood of the vulnerable Olympian, the lamb offers its power of deliverance through the sacrifice of its own blood and the inspiration of a personal testimony. The news and provision of this unique power of deliverance is so inspiring that the Christian Olympian is no longer intimidated by the accusatory breathings from the dragon. Personal loss of life is no longer a deterrent to entering the Christian Race. This is entirely due to the wonderful power that is supplied by the precious blood of the Lamb of God.

The stage has been set for the most spectacular showdown of in the drama of mankind's deliverance from a sinful world. The entrance and interjection of the Lamb presents a contrast of themes. On one hand the dragon is cast down with torturous power against the inhabitants of the earth, but on the other hand, the Lamb of God steps in to offer power and deliverance from the fires of oppression. On one hand the inhabitants of the earth are the recipients of misery and woe, but on the other hand there are shouts of joy because the devil's time for affliction is running short. On one hand, the wrath of the dragon is very great, but on the other hand, the eternal deliverance of the Christian is immensely greater.

Dragon Fury

When one considers the original stature of Lucifer, it is truly amazing to see how far he has fallen.

"How art thou fallen from heaven, O Lucifer, son of the morning? How art thou cut down to the ground, which dist weaken the nations" (Isa 14:12)?

"...Thou sealest up the sum, full of wisdom, and perfect in beauty. Thou wast in Eden the Garden of God; every precious stone was thy covering, the sardius, topaz, and the diamond, the beryl, the onyx, and the jasper, the sapphire, the carbuncle, and gold: the workmanship of thy tabrets and of thy pipes was prepared in thee in the day that thou wast created" (Ezek 28:11-13).

"Thou art the anointed cherub that covereth; and I have set thee so: thou wast upon the holy mountain of God; thou hast walked up and down in the midst of the stones of fire." Thou wast perfect in thy ways from the day that thou wast created, till iniquity was found in thee" (Eze 28:14,15).

"Thine heart was lifted up because of thy beauty, thou has corrupted thy wisdom by reason of thy brightness: I will cast thee to the ground, I will lay thee before kings, that they may behold thee" (Eze 28:17).

"Thou hast defiled the sanctuary by the multitude of the iniquity of thy traffic; therefore I will bring forth a fire from the midst of thee, it shall devour thee, and I will bring thee to ashes upon the earth in the sight of all

them that behold thee. All they that know thee among the people shall be astonished at thee: thou shalt be a terror, and never shalt thou be any more" (Eze 28:18).

Old age, disfigurement and death are some of the embittering elements of life on earth that remind us of the ravages and wages of sin. Though we may be stung by the lethal darts of sin, yet there is a golden strand of hope that reminds us of the possibility of change when we enter the Christian race. The Christian's hope is the hope of transformation from mortal to immortality, and from mortal body to a glorious body. Satan, on the other hand, has no such hope. The word hope is a futile and unrealistic addition to his vocabulary. Because there is no hope for his eternal reconciliation there is the venting of his utter fury.

Before His departure and return to be with His Father, Jesus anointed and established twelve apostles who would continue the spreading of the gospel in His absence. The growth of that newly established church has multiplied exponentially. Today the Christian church has expanded to approximately 2.1 billion members. It is upon every one of these members that the Dragon has targeted his fury. Jesus is the primary target of the dragon; however, due to the impossibility of personally reaching or defeating Jesus, the dragon vents his anger on the people who are most precious to Jesus. The church at large has been his target, but latterly, the target has been the remnant members of the church.

To be a successful Christian Olympian demands the successful transformation from an old and objectionable personality into a personality that is acceptable to Jesus. In his letter to the citizens of Rome, the apostle Paul emphasised the need for change. He pleaded; *"Don't pattern your life after this world, but let God transform you from the inside out and give you a new way of thinking"* (Rom 12:2CW). Because the dragon is aware of the power of a mind that has been successfully renewed by Jesus, he has continually executed a systematic series of disruptions for the purpose of contaminating the change process that has been initiated by Jesus.

When one considers the names that have been attributed to Lucifer after his fall, those names betray a certain behaviour that is expected of him in his opposition to the remnant. The obvious patterns of behaviour are hatred, malice, malevolence, misrepresentation, injury and death. A subtle and unassuming strategy that is used successfully is the mass influx of people. Whereas the intended transformation that Jesus desires calls for personal and individual commitment, The dragon often employs a strategy that appears to enhance fairness and democracy.

Since the goal of the church is to evangelise the world and encourage everyone to become a Christian Olympian, the dragon employs a strategy that deliberately assist the growth strategy of the church, but inserts contamination in the process. Jesus can only save a church that is spotless and without wrinkles, therefore when the dragon cannot defeat the Christian Olympian by overtly vicious stratagems, he acquires success by strategically placing his agents in the church and thereby negatively influence the church from the inside – flooding the church.

A subtle example of this strategy was used effectively when King David attempted to move ark from the house of Abinadab back into its rightful place in Jerusalem. Due to the carelessness of the prophet Eli the recklessness of his sons, and the presumption of the leaders of Israel that the presence of the ark on the battlefield would assist them in their victory against the Philistines, the Ark was captured by the enemy. The magnitude of their loss to the Philistines was leveraged by the use of one word; Ichabod – The glory has departed. Having been displaced from its abode for twenty years, one man expressed unanimous effort to restore the treasured vessel to its rightful place.

The zeal of King David to facilitate the return the Ark to its rightful place was matched by the enthusiasm of the nation. In a move of transparency and democracy, David sought counsel from every sector of the land and secured their unanimous support for his ambitions. There was not a dissenting voice to be heard, yet the sole voice that mattered was not consulted. As at the time of its initial displacement the leaders did not enquire of the Lord, so in this instance they failed to enquire of the Lord.

When the swelling voices of the nation agreed in unanimous approval, no one dared to assume that their ambitions would engender error and attract tragedy. Tragedy struck when Uzzah, one of the trusted sons of Abinadab, in order to prevent the Ark from falling, reached out and touched the Ark. Judgement from heaven was swift and lethal.

Immediately a cry was heard as Uzzah fell dead. in response to his priestly diligence to protect the Ark, Uzzah fell foul of a critical divine mandate. No human hand was supposed to touch the Ark. In fact, the Ark was not supposed to be transported by cart as the Philistines had initiated, it was meant to be carried by two poles, on the shoulders of four priests. In fear and dread King David diverted the Ark to the house of Obededom, and there it rested for three months.

Meanwhile, King David and the priests were dutiful in searching to assess their error. Upon the realisation that there was a prescribed divine mandate for transporting the Ark, coupled with the reports that the house of Obededom was being notably blessed as a result of hosting the Ark, David hastily, but carefully, applied the correct procedure and thus achieved his ambition.

Along with the mass of people who gave him their support, David learned that mass consensus and goodwill cannot substitute for thus saith the Lord. Indeed, the prophet Samuel conveyed that message to King Saul with the words; ... *"Behold, to obey is better than sacrifice, and to hearken than the fat of rams..."* (I Sam 15:22). This brings us back to an apparent anomaly, namely, the transmutation from dragon to serpent and the massive release of water from the mouth of the serpent. Satan is the master of disguises. He is able to adapt and trans-mutate into the creature that suits his purpose. Thus, the dragon in his adaptation causes water to flood the church in order to liquidate the potency of the message of the church.

The residue of the Tsunami that struck Japan on 11th March 2011 conveyed the power of water to destroy and transport its destruction. The Japan Tsunami transported houses and cars from their normal positions and left them in heaps of chaos. Boats and ships were tossed inland and literally left high and dry. Picture of boats left on the tops of houses and other buildings painted a picture of incredulity. Thus, flooding is not only capable of submerging and drowning, it is also capable of transporting and displacing. Christian Olympians must be aware of the power and potential strategies of the dragon.

The history of the Christian church during the period of the dark ages witnessed a church that was at the mercy of vicious and depraved minds. Baseless crime plagued the land as the candlelight of dignity and grace was extinguished by the agents of violence and debauchery. The dragon unleashed a flood of violence against the church in an effort to permanently extinguish its light from the entire earth. The leap of change that is witnessed today is due to the assistance that the church has received from pivotal places. We are no longer living in the dark ages, however, the church is still subject to attacks from the same dragon. Today the Christian Olympian must be aware of the fact that the dragon is wroth with the remnant residents of the church. That remnant would include every member of the human race who chooses to be associated with the name and followers of Jesus Christ.

Typically, the word remnant refers to the left over or residue of the main body of substance or fabric that once was. The remnant of the seed of the church represents those who bare and maintain the marks of the imprint of the major or original beliefs of the original church. The dragon is not intimidated by the diluted beliefs of masses who bear the name of Christianity, however, he is highly stressed by a small group who maintain the potency of Jesus' original teachings in their daily lifestyle. This small group of people are identified as commandment keepers and as those who unashamedly testify of the power of God within their lives. In essence, the same reason for which Peter and John were reprimanded in Acts ch 4&5 is the same reason for which the dragon is wroth with the followers of Jesus today. The modern Christian Olympian must be aware that the wroth of the dragon is merely a description of a greater response that is swelling like a tsunami within the people of the earth.

The dragon is not just angry, he is converting his anger into full scale warfare that is intended to sever or disrupt the connection between Christians and their God. The Ten Commandments that were handed to Moses upon Mt Sinai are the same commandments that cause great anxiety to the dragon. Thus, those who assume and teach that the commandments have been changed or diluted are sadly mistaken. The same commandments which were written by the finger of God are the ones that will fortify the Christians against the deceptions and wiles of the dragon. It is the love and passion of the Christian that will hold him or her in the midst of the storms of life.

Agents of Fury

The desire and decision to become a follower of Jesus Christ is a commitment of admirable faith. Whilst Christianity has experienced its glory days, the best and the worst of the Christian experiences are yet to come. Foremost in the minds of Christians is the return of their Lord and saviour and the inauguration of a new era where there will be a total absence of satanic interference. In as much as that will be an era of total glory, the dragon will unleash his greatest anti-Christian forces in an attempt to thwart the accomplishment of those lofty aspirations. Myriads of charges and allegations have been attributed to the mastermind of global evil, yet he remains invisible to the human eye. Caricature forms of creatures have been attributed to him, yet there is not a photo of him to be seen. Some have even acclaimed that there is no such person as a devil or Satan.

THE DEVIL IS DEAD

Men don't believe in a devil now
As their fathers used to do
They've forced the door of the broadest creed
To let his majesty through
There isn't a print of his cloven foot
Or a fiery dart from his bow
To be found in the earth or the air today
For the world has voted so
They say he doesn't go round about
As a roaring lion now
But whom shall we hold responsible
for the everlasting row.
To be heard in home and church and state
To the earth's remotest bound
If the devil, by a unanimous vote
Is nowhere to be found?
Who is mixing the fatal draught?
That palsies heart and brain
And loads the bier of each passing year
With ten hundred thousand slain?
Who blights the bloom of the land today?

With the fiery breath of hell
If the devil isn't and never was?
Won't someone rise and tell?
Who dogs the steps of the toiling saint?
And digs the pit for his feet?
Who sows the tears in the years of time?
Wherever God sows his wheat?
The devil was voted not to be,
And of course the saying is true;
But who is doing the kind of work that the devil used to do?
Won't somebody step to the front forthwith?
And make his bow and show
How the frauds and crimes of a single day spring up?
We want to know
The devil was fairly voted out
And of course the devil's gone
But simple people want to know
Who carries his business on?

Since the Devil or the Dragon is nowhere to be seen by the human eye, the thirteenth chapter of the book of Revelation offers some assistance to our quest to understand and identify the agents of fury. Chief among the agents of fury that are identified in chapter thirteen is a blasphemous beast. This blasphemous beast is:

- Dragon empowered.
- Given a seat by the dragon.
- Receives its commission from the dragon.

The book of Revelation is widely regarded as a prophetic book. Many phrases and words used in the book are therefore used within prophetic context. The use of and referral to the word "*beast*" must be understood in prophetic context. The book of Daniel, which many regard as the Old Testament's precursor to the book of Revelation, gives a plain interpretation of the meaning of the word beast when used in prophetic context.

In the seventh chapter of the book which bears his name, Daniel experienced dreams and visions during which he saw four great winds striving upon the sea and four great beasts come up from the sea. Daniel's description of the four beasts was a remarkable description of the future events of geographic super powers depicted in animal symbolism. The first beast was described as a Lion with eagle's wings. This Lion stood on its feet like a man and was given a man's heart. The second beast was a Bear with three ribs in its mouth. The third beast was a Leopard with four wings on its back and four heads protruding from its body. The description of the fourth beast was not so specific; however, it was described as dreadful and strong. The fourth beast was given iron teeth and ten horns. With its teeth it devoured and broke in pieces and with its feet it stamped the residue of its victims. Critical contribution is given to the understanding of the used of the word beast. "…*The fourth beast shall be the fourth kingdom upon the earth….*" (Dan 7:23).

As in the book of Daniel, the use of the word "beast" in the book of Revelation, in prophetic context, refers to kingdoms, governments or earthly ruling organisations. When the book of Revelation refers to a blasphemous beast, it is referring to an earthly government or political organisation that openly blasphemes the name of God. The definition given to the word blasphemy is: "*.. abuse of or contempt for God or sacred things,*" *or;* "*any speech or action contemptuous of something deemed sacred.*"[1]

During the days of Jesus' ministry, popular Jewish thought was that anyone found guilty of blasphemy was guilty of the highest crime and worthy of death. Thus the continual insistence of Jesus to forgive the sins of those whom He healed and the final claim that He was the Christ, resulted in a constant claim of blasphemy against Him. It was the alleged claim of blasphemy that prompted the high priest to rip His clothes and pronounce that He was guilty of death (Mk 14:61-64).

The charge of blasphemy, whilst falsely and incorrectly applied to Jesus, is a crime of the highest spiritual order. It is no wonder, therefore, that an organisation that is sponsored by the dragon for the purpose of opposing God – wears this inscription on the crowns of its heads of governments. The clear inference is that opposition against God is the clear intent and objective of the last beast. This last beast has used its mouth to speak blasphemous words against God, against the name of God, against the tabernacle of God and against the inhabitants of heaven. The Christian Olympian must not be vague in his or her understanding of the need to avoid being spiritually aligned with the inhabitants of this spiritual and blasphemous political/religious government.

Whilst the era of the dark ages was a violent and wretched era against the Christian Church, the future era of opposition from the dragon will inaugurate an era of spiritual and political opposition that will lead to the final confrontation between Christendom and the dragon. The events of the future will be both sinister and insidious. The invisible dragon, who is the devil himself, will empower a religious organisation to coerce and attract political and martial support and leverage from another supporting government who commands political and martial power. True worship is the response of voluntary reverence and adoration towards an independent person or object. The worship of God is the objective of the Christian. The dragon, who is opposed to the spiritual allegiance that is directed toward God, has orchestrated a system of opposition that is intended to duplicate and mandate that which God is now receiving from voluntary worshippers.

The crisis of the future will be an outpouring of vitriolic jealousy and envy whose roots reach back to the opposition of Lucifer in heaven warring against the Godhead. In as much as he was able to coerce and deceive one third of the heavenly host, Lucifer, now Satan, will command, via military force, that all the world exert allegiance toward the beast, hence worshipping Satan himself. It will indeed be both sinister and insidious, however, it represents an era when Christians will stand up and stand out.

The inhabitants of the world have witnessed a rapid and dramatic change in the financial and political fortunes of governments and nations. Organisations, governments and nations that were assumed to be stable and secure are tumbling and crumbling. Political and fiscal instability appears to be the crisis of the day. The line that connects the troubled hotspots of the world have darted through Iraq, Japan, USA, Iceland, Australia, Greece, Egypt, Libya, Syria and the nations of Europe. The world has witnessed floods, tsunamis, civil wars and financial meltdown. It appears as though a Ferris wheel of crisis has enveloped the earth, and no one is sure where it will all end. In the midst of extreme despair when the world will search for solutions, it is certain that the dragon will usurp the adversity of humanity to assert his recommendations to institute reconciliation.

The tragedy of any assistance that is offered by the dragon is that it will be via the auspices of a beast. No matter how well a beast is trained or attempts made to domesticate such animal, there still remains that internal capacity to rip, devour or destroy. When a political power or government is empowered by the dragon, it will eventually resort to beast like behaviour. It will rip and devour its citizens.

Some current and future Christians will live to experience the power of government sponsored terrorism. In other words, the violence against Christians that is reported from Muslim and communist countries will also be reflected in future behaviour in so-called Christian friendly countries. The dragon is at war, not just with God, but against those who worship God. The essence of that war will be the pressure, insistence and coercion of political organisations that all nations pay homage to the specific religious organisation that will be identified.

In addition to the beasts that have already been identified the dragon will utilise the assistance of another beast that is lamb-like in appearance yet speak with the vocals of a dragon. This beast/government will exercise all the power of the previous beast/government that exercised coercive force to secure worship and allegiance. This lamb-like beast/government will not seek worship on behalf of itself; it will instigate worship on behalf of the previous beast/government. There are exceptional instances in the world when megalomaniacs have demanded worship from their citizens; however, none have attracted support from a global superpower to assist their quest. It will be most surprising, therefore, that in an era when international alliances are calling for the overthrow of despots and the reform of political incorrectness, a beast/government of major international stature will be spearheading a similar dictate. Whist such future action will be surprising, it must be understood that the power behind such movement is the power of the dragon. As fictional as this may sound, this is the reality that will confront the future Christian.

Whilst in the wilderness after His baptism, one the three temptations that the Devil submitted to Jesus was the enticement to bow down and worship him (Matt 4:9). The Devils is hungry for global worship. In this future event where there will be a global thrust for individual and filial devotion, demand for compliance will utilise the threat of the penalty of death. The dragon, working through the agency of the Lamb-like beast will invoke a draconian mandate.

"And he causeth all, both small and great, rich and poor, free and bond, to receive a mark in their right hand, or in their foreheads: And no man might buy or sell, save he that had the mark of the beast, or the number of his name. Here is wisdom. Let him that hath understanding count the number of the beast: for it is the number of a man; and his number is Six hundred three score and six" (Rev 13:16-18).

It is incongruous that whilst we live in an era when the human rights of the disenfranchised are being championed by international agencies, a government of superpower statue will exercise authority that tramples on such freedom, on behalf of a religious/beast/government.

Due to the severity of this prophecy and the interpretation that is applied, the reader and the Christian Olympian must be aware of this divine caveat.

"If a man or a woman who claims to be a prophet predicts something in the name of the Lord, and whatever he or she said does not happen, then that message was not from the Lord. Whatever that person said was his or her own idea" (Deut 18:22CW).

With that caveat in place we return to the wisdom of the word. The wisdom of the word of God declares that the ultimate fatal mark that can be applied to the Olympic Christian is the MARK of the BEAST. Several points are noteworthy, namely:

- The application of the Mark of the Beast is future in occurrence.
- The instigation of the mark will be sponsored by a beast / government of significant global status.
- The legalisation of the mark impinges upon the rights of citizens to buy or sell.
- The number of the mark is 666.

- Whoever receives this mark will automatically be declaring allegiance to the dragon – to Satan.
- The mark will be identifiable on the forehead or in the right hand.
- The names of the recipient of this mark will not be written in heaven's book of life.
- Whosoever receives this mark is most unwise.
- Whosoever receives this mark will not enter heaven.
- The war against the dragon is championed by the Lamb of God.
- The outcome and winner is assured

Notes

1. Clarence L. Barnhart, <u>The World Book Dictionary</u>. Volume One A-K. World Book Inc. Chicago. London. Sydney. Toronto. p.211

6

THE LAMB IS NO MASCOT

One of the notable features that is often included in the promotion of modern Olympic games is the introduction of an Olympic mascot. Mascots have been created and introduced as a catalyst for generating enthusiasm and interest in the games. Some athletes and spectators may even have worn their reproduced mascot as a talisman or good luck charm. Whilst beasts of unique description have been featured on the front line of the dragon's aggression against the remnant church of God, one innocuous creature appears as the symbol of victory for the entire cause of God. That creature is a lamb.

It hardly seems right that after the aggressive display of beasts of ferocity and the explicit threats of death by the dragon and his agents, the symbol of God's victory over the dragon is portrayed by a lamb. On the literal aggressive prairie of the Masai Mara, a lamb would be a mere snack for the parching appetites of a pride of lions, yet, here portrayed before the most ferocious aggression of the dragon stands a lamb. This is not even a lamb with horns, it is a lamb of symbolic innocence. However, let not your hope melt away in defeatism due to the powerlessness of your understanding of earthly symbols. The potency of this lamb's power of deliverance spans the entire gamut of humanity's existence upon the planet earth. At the pivotal moment when all appears hopeless and lost, the Lamb appears standing on Mt Zion, the mountain of victory.

The Substitute Lamb

Until a person develops a personal acquaintance with God, he or she remains oblivious to the devastative nature of sin to warp the mind and deceive the intellect. The impact that sin has on the human mind is that it disrupts the mind from its originally intended path of spiritual progression. Sin perverts and blocks spiritual understanding. Long before mankind was aware of sin's impact, God had a plan in place for their entire redemption. Despite His everlasting love for Adam and Eve, when they committed sin in the Garden of Eden, Jehovah could not erase the wages and consequences of sin, however, He had already set in place a plan that would counter the impact.

The phrase *"from the foundation of the world"* is understood to refer to events or plans made before man and woman were created. Thus, before the entrance of sin into the world, and due to their knowledge of possibilities, God the Father and Jesus chose us before the foundation of the world (Eph 1:4). The decision was made and accepted, that Jesus would redeem mankind from sin buy the personal sacrifice of Himself (Heb 9:26). Had this plan not been in place before the intrusion of sin, Adam and Eve would have died on the very day that they ate of the forbidden fruit. The grace of God was demonstrated by the continuance of their lives, however, God brought the knowledge of the plan of salvation to their awareness. The simple essence of the plan was that, for each day where they committed sin - they would sacrifice a lamb and offer that sacrifice to God in remission for their sin.

This was a plan that was set in place from *"the foundation of the world,"* therefore any one who deviated from the provision for redemption from sin was indeed missing the mark. The introduction of the lamb as a substitute for the death of the sinner was intended as a substitute and a deterrent. Cain's decision to offer to God the best of the fruits of the ground instead of the lamb that was required was eternally deficient and disrespectful. The decision of Abel to offer a lamb did not necessarily mean that he understood the full significance of his offering, nevertheless, due to his obedience alone, his offering was accepted.

The simple sacrifice that was requested of Cain and Abel was in stark contrast to monumental request that was required by Abraham on Mount Moriah. God spoke to Abraham declaring; *"...take now thy son, thine only son Isaac, whom thou lovest, and get thee into the land of Moriah; and offer him there for a burnt offering upon one of the mountains which I will tell thee of"* (Gen 22:2). As Isaac accompanied his father to the place that was designated by God, upon arrival, he expressed his observation of one notable

absence from his father's intended plan. *"My father,"* he said, *"…
Behold the fire and the wood: but where is the lamb for a burnt offering"*
(Gen 22:7). The answer given was both instructive for the
moment and prophetic for the duration of mankind's existence
upon earth.

*"And Abraham said, My son, God will provide himself a lamb for a
burnt offering"* (Gen 22:8).

When the altar was set and no lamb was in sight, Isaac being
unaware of God's instructions to his father, was truly surprised
when his father bound his hands and feet and laid him on the altar
of wood to be slain as the intended sacrifice. As Abraham lifted
his hand with the knife, intending to do as God commanded, a
voice from heaven spoke and said; *"Abraham, Abraham,… lay not
thine hand upon the lad, neither do thou anything unto him: for I know
that thou fearest God, seeing thou hast not withheld thy son, thine only son
from me"* (Gen 22:11,12).

When we progress to the crucifixion of Jesus upon Mount Calvary,
we witness the sacrifice of the Son of God without interference
from His father. Thus as God, He offered Himself as a sacrifice,
but as Son he submitted Himself to be sacrificed. Hence we hear
the cry of the son; *"My God, My God, why hast thou forsaken me"*
(Matt 27:46). God the Father could not do anything less with His
son Jesus than Abraham would have done with his son Isaac.

It was a tremendous price to pay for the ransom of humanity. This tremendous sacrifice demands the response of equal understanding and respect.

"Forasmuch as ye know that ye were not redeemed with corruptible things, as silver and Gold, … But with the precious blood of Christ, as of a lamb without blemish and without spot.. Who verily was foreordained before the foundation of the world, but was manifested in these last times for you" (I Pet 1:18-20).

The Lamb Eulogised by Isaiah

Throughout the passage of the centuries the understanding and embracing of the sacrificing of a lamb as a pardon from personal sin has not been positively reflected in the lives of the nation of Israel. Abel had respect for the will of God and brought a lamb for his sacrifice. Cain, on the other had responded with a self-willed attitude and brought what he wanted instead of what God had requested.

Cain's attitude represented the majority of Israel who would follow in his footsteps by disobeying the will of God and offering something other than that which was requested. Often if they did not bring the required sacrifice they brought the correct offering, but with an incorrect attitude of heart. If there were times when the Lord rejected the correct sacrifice of the sinner, his rejection could be interpreted to understand that attitude determines altitude.

Whilst the Lord was specific in the sacrifice that was appointed, He was equally interested in in the attitude of the sinner. A mere offering without sincere repentance was grossly inadequate. The words of the prophet Samuel to King Saul were therefore applicable to all of Israel. *"Hath the Lord as a great a delight in burnt offerings and sacrifices, as in obeying the voice of the Lord? Behold, to obey is better than sacrifice, and to hearken than the fat of rams"* (I Sam 15:22). The behaviour of Israel toward her God was as a promiscuous bride, indeed like a prostitute. Whilst prophets were appointed to rebuke and correct their behaviour and steer the people in the right direction none were truly successful. Despite their lamentable spiritual failure as a nation the words of one prophet were heard to declare the inevitable appearance of the nation's redeemer.

The words of the prophet Isaiah employed a strange mixture of contextual vocabulary that reached back, examined then current national behaviour and peered into the future to paint a picture of the future embodiment of a national emancipatory symbol. Isaiah's words declared that He is coming! Since the time of Adam and Eve's eviction from the Garden of Eden the descendants of Adam had been looking for the promised Redeemer. In chapter fifty three of his book, Isaiah wrote approximately seven hundred years before his birth that the Messiah would be a suffering servant.

In as much as the sacrificial system was an inseparable part of the daily life of Israel, the treatment that would be meted out to the chosen one for whom they waited would be unbelievable. Who would believe this report? The person on whom the report is focussed is described by the personal masculine pronoun "*He*" no less than twenty four times. Isaiah's report concludes that "*He*" would be caught in the middle, between His Father's desire and His people's brutality. The suffering servant about whom Isaiah wrote was understood to be a real person, hence the repeated use of the personal pronoun. However, the allegorical use of the word "lamb" in one verse is sufficient to bridge the synapse between the Old Testament sacrificial Lamb and the victorious Lamb that stands on Mount Zion in the book of Revelation.

The relevance of the Lamb to the Olympic Christian is due to the need to understand and embrace the spiritual history of the One who is going to be his/her deliverer when beasts and dragon collude to destroy the Christian. Isaiah significantly declares that there is a collaborative divine involvement that places the "*He*" in the line of fire of vicious people and ultimately causes "*He*", the Lamb, to be sacrificed.

The arm of the Lord, being separate from "*He*," indicates that God the Father and consequently God the Holy Spirit were collaborators expressing their agreement for "*Him*" (another use of the personal pronoun – used nine times to refer to the Lamb) to undergo such inhuman abuse. If we would employ the usage of terminology applied to a card player, we would have to say that God the Father and The Holy Spirit were revealing their hands. Through the ministry of the prophet Isaiah, to whom they had given this divine revelation, they were clearly stating, in graphic details, the manner in which the deliverer of Israel, the Lamb, would be treated.

There are many servants who benefit from the benevolent generosity of their masters; however, Isaiah wrote that this servant would be the object of numerous sufferings. He would not enjoy any personal benefits of charm or physical appeal. He would be despised and rejected by many. His people would turn their backs on Him as though He had no value. He would be chastised, beaten with many stripes, wounded, bruised, pierced, oppressed, afflicted, under the misguidance of false accusation, and finally executed. His misguided people would largely incorrectly assume that He was smitten, afflicted and rejected by God. In an act of contradictory behaviour, they who needed His emancipation would wander as sheep without a shepherd.

One verse in this chapter, verse seven, links the allegorical lamb to the servant emancipator. "... *He is brought as a lamb to the slaughter, and as a sheep before her shearers is dumb, so he openeneth not his mouth*" (Isa 53:7). Thousands of years had witnessed the slaying and sacrificing of lambs, prefiguring his coming, yet he would live in the midst of his people and they would all be blind to his identity. He would be lamb like in their presence. He would suffer the indignity of being physically violated, unjustly maligned and separated from his earthly heritage as a common criminal. The power of ten thousand angels was at his beckoning yet, He avoided the temptation to access any element of divine supernatural power. Given the power that was available and his refusal to access any of that power for his personal deliverance, he was truly lamb like.

He was led as a lamb by His Father. The actions of His Father represent a unique and antitypical mixture of love and enmity. On the one hand He was utterly loved by His Father, but on the other hand, He embodied within Himself the ultimate strength and opposition of two opposing worlds. He was the only man that was born of the seed of the Holy Spirit, therefore He embodied a mixture that was uniquely formed to represent both earth and heaven. The redemption of mankind needed someone who fitted his profile, and he was the only one. As one born of a woman, he represented humanity, but also as one born of the Holy Spirit, He represented the Godhead.

The redemption of mankind needed a human sacrifice that superseded the cumulative sacrifices of all the lambs that were slain. The stature of the Gods needed someone of their equal to present himself as that ultimate sacrifice. Jesus, as the son of Mary and also the son of God was the only person who fulfilled the credentials that were sufficient for both worlds. Therefore, it pleased the Father to bruise him, and to allow him to be presented as a sacrificial offering for the sins of mankind. He had committed no violent act, no deceit was found in His mouth, and He himself testified that; "...*the prince of this world cometh and hath nothing in me*" (Jn 14:30). His human reputation was flawless and thus acceptable to the Father.

Divine pleasure would demonstrate the strange act of God the Father going beyond the actions of Abraham by allowing His son to be submitted as a sacrificial lamb. Whilst death is not the pleasure of God, in this act of sacrifice the Father demonstrated His satisfaction. Given the acceptance of His Father, Jesus, the sacrificial lamb, could also look back at His deeds and be satisfied that they were worth the ultimate travail and separation from His Father. At the height of his travail He could demonstrate the power to forgive, even in the most extreme circumstances. Despite being on the receiving end of extreme cruelty He could still say; "*Father, forgive them; for they know not what they do*" (Lk 23:34). He then crowned His lamb-like behaviour without a word of retaliation as he breathed His last breath and comment with the words: "*Father, into thy hands, I commend my spirit*" (Lk 23:46).

The prophetic words of Isaiah would realise their fulfilment in the writings of the four gospels. As if guided by a hand from the deep past, Matthew, Mark Luke and John would catalogue the deeds of a Saviour who gave Himself as a complete catalyst for the social and spiritual ills of Israel and the world. From His humble beginnings in a manger of Bethlehem, the Lamb would grow and develop the capacity to challenge a roaring lion. Isaiah, in chapter 61 of his books revealed the secret of the lamb's enabling power. The Spirit of God would anoint the Lamb of God with power to maximise his ministry across all social and spiritual spheres.

In a world that was dominated by Roman power, the anointed Lamb emerged on the scene to give hope to the least, the smallest and the hopeless. Whilst his words delivered hope and comfort, his touch healed and liberated. A dishevelled society rapidly grew in confidence and even dared to openly celebrate him as the king of the Jews. The very positive attributes that catapulted him into favour are the same attributes that engendered disfavour and ultimate condemnation. In spite of the fact that the leaders of the nation were largely blinded to their own spiritual deficiencies the wisdom and vision of the Lamb of God remained focused on the task for which he was born. Weak and emaciated, the Lamb could declare upon crucifixion's completion; *"It is finished"* (Jn 19:30)!

The Heralded Lamb

The strategic methods of God are beyond comprehension. His

methods often defy and confound normal human logic. The redemption of the world though the beneficence of a sacrificial lamb appeared to be uncomprehended by the majority, yet one man from the vantage tower of his own ministry, looked for, spotted and heralded the arrival of the Lamb of God upon the scene that would eventually lead to his ultimate sacrifice. The prophet Isaiah had clearly detailed the extent of the sufferings of the Lamb of God but, in addition, he announced the role and purpose of one who would precede him as a forerunner.

The prophecy of Isaiah clearly announced the coming of a wilderness reformer who would prepare the way of the Lord by straitening every crooked way and levelling every mountainous terrain. After the forerunner would have completed his task, Isaiah declared that "*the glory of the Lord shall be revealed, and all flesh shall see it together*" (Isa 40:5). John the Baptist arrived on the scene as though he had read the script. His preaching was so strident that, in addition to the genuine listeners to his messages of reform, the Pharisees sent their spies to enquire who he was. His response was unequivocally linked to the message of Isaiah Chapter 40. "*He said, I am the voice of one crying in the wilderness, Make straight the way of the Lord...*" (Jn 1:23).

Whilst they may not have repented or agreed with the sentiments of his preaching, their minds clearly synchronised with the words of Isaiah, therefore eyebrows must have raised on the next day when John seeing Jesus coming declared; *"Behold the Lamb of God which taketh away the sin of the world"* (Jn 1:29). In addition to his announcement of the Lamb of God, the language of John highlighted his connection with his divine commissioner.

A replay of those brief events and an identification of the main players suggest the importance of that heralded moment. In reverse order; John saw Jesus and identified Him as the Lamb of God. John saw the Holy Spirit descending in the form of a dove and lighted upon the shoulder of Jesus. Jesus and the Holy Spirit being identified, the third remaining person was undoubtedly God the Father. The Father did indeed confirm His own identification with a voice that was audible to John saying; *"This is my beloved Son, in whom I am well pleased"* (Matt 3:17).

The fact that the heralded moment made little impact upon the minds of the Judeans did not diminish the significance of the arrival of the Lamb of God or the application of His ministry to the region and the world. Jesus the Lamb of God was here and the ministering works of the Lamb would undoubtedly follow.

The collective events of that heralded moment should suggest to the Olympic Christian, the need to pay attention to apparent minor matters of spiritual import. Jesus, the Lamb of God was not introduced to this world in ostentatious trappings, yet His arrival meant all or nothing to the entire world. The significance of that moment could not be diluted by slanderous allegations regarding His birth and parentage. Likewise, the legitimacy of the prophecies that foretell His return to this earth will not diminish the reality of the day when, we like John the Revelator, will see the Lamb of God standing victoriously on Mt Zion.

John's was a singular voice, but on the day of eternal deliverance from sin, the voice of John will be accompanied by multitudes who will hail the Lamb of God as the final victor over the powers of sin. That multitude of voices needs to include the voice of every Olympic Christian.

The Fulfilled Lamb

The ministry of Jesus was constantly confronted with bigotry, ostracism and malignment from the very people to whom he came to minister. The prophecy of Isaiah specifically stated that *"He shall see the travail of His soul, and He shall be satisfied"* (Isa 53:11). The concept of personal satisfaction appears to be stridently contradicted by the words of disappointment uttered by Jesus Himself. *"O Jerusalem, Jerusalem, thou that killest the prophets, and stonest them which are sent unto thee, how often would I have gathered thy children together, even as a hen gathereth her chicks under her wings, and ye would not! Behold your house is left unto you desolate"* (Matt 23:37,38). This statement uttered by Jesus hardly seems to convey a spirit of satisfaction.

This was He who traded His throne in heaven for a stall in a manger. He relinquished his palatial dwellings and existed on earth like a nomad. Foxes had holes and birds the security of their nests, but the son of God had no dwelling to call his own. Was He really satisfied? The measure of satisfaction of which Isaiah spoke should not be compared with the accumulation or ownership of human assets. As monarch in heaven He owned all the assets of earth, however, the vital gem that was lacking from his regal possession was the unsalable companionship of humanity free from the ravages of sin. It was due to his objective to save humanity to the uttermost that he prostrated himself to the least of humanity.

When Jesus touched and revived a leper and raised the dead back to life He was demonstrating the depth to which He extended Himself for the sake of lost humanity. Both the leper and the dead were considered untouchables and unredeemable, yet Jesus demonstrated that human degradation has no depths that divinity cannot reach and reconcile. His ministry to Nichodemus demonstrated that human intelligence, at its best, is ignorant of the incomprehensible methods of salvation. For three and a half years Jesus ministered to a range of people that span the gamut from the dead and bereaved to the pious and wealthy. In between those contrasting ranges was the caption of a host of personalities who benefitted from the fact that a human lamb was to be slain on their behalf.

Divine satisfaction should not be measured by human instruments but by the accomplishments of divine objectives. Once again Isaiah's ministry was pivotal in prophesying the objectives of the coming messiah. Jesus confirmed Isaiah's predictions when He stood in a Nazarene synagogue, read the respective passage from the book of Isaiah and, after taking His seat declared, *"This day is this scripture fulfilled in your ears"* (Lk 4:21). Seven objectives projected the remit of His divine assignment:

- Anointed to preach good tidings to the meek.
- Bind up the broken hearted.
- Proclaim liberty to the captives.
- Recover the sight of the blind.
- Open the prison doors of the captives.
- Proclaim the acceptable year of the Lord.
- Comfort all that mourned.

These objectives reflected the comprehensive divine applicators that were necessary to address the range of suffering that humanity was experiencing. There was a need for a Redeemer with a human touch, one that could identify with and be counted as one of the people. This human affiliation was merely to serve as a human magnate, its practice had no salvific value within itself. What was ultimately needed was the application of a remedy that could and would eradicate sin for all eternity.

The practice of the Levitical sacrificial system was merely the writing of a cheque that had to be underwritten by the fulfilment of one lamb that was truly unblemished. Jesus the Lamb of God, came to accomplish that purpose. When Jesus said, after reading the passage from Isaiah; *"This day is this scripture fulfilled in your ears"* (Lk 4:21); what He was really saying was - I am here to fulfil the prophecy. Absolute fulfilment could only be satisfied when He had completed his ministry and received validation from His Father. There was a long way to go and multiple obstacles to avoid before that would become a reality. Satan, the prince of this world, His arch enemy, would instigate every act of interference in order to secure one act of deviation from His immaculate ministry.

Whilst all of the objectives of his three and a half years of ministry were commendable, they pale in insignificance to the one act that was pivotal to the entire redemption process. An impeccable performance was necessary in order for the Lamb to be slain; therefore Satan baited Jesus from the outset of His ministry to the very end. His arsenal of temptations ranged from the temptation of appetite when Jesus was led by the Spirit into the wilderness, to the temptation to secure Himself from personal injury when He was arrested. Jesus refused to satiate his hunger by rebuking the devil with the words; *"Man shall not live by bread alone, but by every word that proceedeth out of the mouth of God"* (Matt 4:4). When the zeal of Peter led him to draw his sword resulting in the severed ear of Malchus, a servant of the high priest, Jesus restored the ear of Mulchus and urged Peter to put away his sword.

The verbal response of Jesus highlighted perfect control in the midst of extreme adversity, but it also highlighted His satisfaction that the objectives of His ministry were being fulfilled. *"Do you think that I cannot call on my Father, and He will at once put at my disposal more than twelve legions of angels? But how then would the Scriptures be fulfilled that say it must happen in this way"* (Matt 26:53,54)? The long road that led to the altar of sacrifice was nearing its end and Jesus, though weary, was satisfied. The prince of this world had examined Him at every stage and found nothing worthy of blame in Him.

The conclusive acts of His ministry were winding to a close. Viscous and inhumane acts of violence were shrouding the fact that the greatest act of salvation was taking place. The Lamb of God was being prepared to be placed on the altar of human sacrifice. As cruel as it was for this degradation to take place, the satisfaction of Jesus was that it only need happen once.

"For Christ also hath once suffered for sins, the just for the unjust, that he might bring us to God, being put to death in the flesh, but quickened by the Spirit" (I Pet 3:18).

Due to the fact that He, Jesus, was offered once, He has made sanctification possible for all mankind.

"So Christ was once offered to bear the sins of many; and unto them that look for him shall he appear the second time without sin unto salvation" (Heb 9:28).

In as much as He came to this earth for the sole purpose of redeeming mankind back to God, the process of securing that redemption had to be precise to the last detail. The final days of His ministry were critical to satisfy the requirements of four significant areas. These areas of focus were:

- The avoidance of sin in any area of His life.
- The shedding and application of His blood.
- None of His bones should be broken.
- The acceptance of His sacrifice by His Father.

The absence of any evidence of sin throughout the life of Jesus resulted in the fabrication of lies that attributed sin to His character. However, it was affirmed that the prince of this world could find nothing in Him.

The method of His death was as important as the reason for His death. Salvation's process could not be accomplished if Jesus died of a stroke or a heart attack. Blood had to be shed on our behalf. The foreshadowing of all the sacrifices that were performed before His death all pointed to the fact that blood makes the atonement possible.

"In all the offerings… atonement is made by the blood, and not by the body. *The body served as a means of sin transfer when the priest ate of the flesh.* *And in all cases the fat was burned on the altar as a sweet savor. But the* *blood accomplished the atonement. And it did this by reason of the life.* *Christ's life, symbolized by the blood, is our salvation."* [1]

When His persecutors placed a crown of thorns upon His head blood flowed down upon His face, but a more significant flow of blood was necessary. Therefore, *"…one of the soldiers with a spear pierced His side and forthwith came there out blood and water"* (Jn 19:34). It was the custom of the Roman soldier to break the legs of their victims in order to hasten their demise. The soldiers broke the legs of the other two victims who were crucified beside Jesus. *"But when they came to Jesus, and saw that he was dead already, they brake not his legs"* (Jn 19:33). This was not mere coincidence; this was the fulfilment of Levitical practice and prophecy. According to the ordinance of the Passover, and the prophetic words of Ps 34:20 the ministry of John confirmed; *"For these things were done, that the scripture should be fulfilled, A bone of him shall not be broken"* (Jn 19:36).

The final stage of His ministry and sacrifice was just as critical as the other stages. The Father was the one who agreed for the sacrifice to take place. The Father was the one who affirmed his pleasure at the way His son had conducted himself and it would be the Father who world confirm the acceptance of a job well done. Whilst Jesus declared, *"It is finished,"* there was still the outstanding approval of His Father. When Mary therefore arrived at the sepulchre on the third day of His death she was confronted by a risen Saviour. No doubt jubilation would have prompted her to embrace him, but he said; *"touch me not for I have not yet ascended to my Father"* (Jn 20:17).

Just as the smoke from the altar of the burning sacrifice in the Levitical system ascendance from The Holy place and wafted over the veil into The Most Holy place, Jesus would make a similar transition. In the old Levitical system, human hands could not intervene between the smoke and its destination. The smoke that ascended from the Holy to the Most Holy place needed the final sanction from the God whose Shekinah Glory dwelt in the Most Holy Place. Jesus, therefore, having risen from the grave and the altar of sacrifice, became the metaphorical smoke from the altar that needed the ultimate approval of his Father.

That approval having been given, Jesus was therefore free to return to this earth with the full rights of divinity regained and the full rights of humanity earned by his sacrifice at Calvary. He, indeed, has been fulfilled and his return to earth to greet and encourage his disciples was also to encourage every human being thereafter that the Lamb of God has been slain for all of our sins and that we can overcome the pressures of this world because of the blood of the Lamb.

The Lamb Transformed and Renewed

After the recorded ascension of Jesus in the book of Acts, there remained a void of information as to his precise whereabouts and his ministry on behalf of humanity. That void of information began to be filled by the book of Hebrews. Jesus came to this world to fulfil a specific mission. The Son of God became incarnate in order to satisfy the requirements for human redemption and once that mission had been accomplished He resumed His former state and position seated beside His Father.

He has not gone to heaven to muse and murmur about the depths of man's depravity. He has returned to heaven to engage in the active and vigorous ministry of interceding on behalf of those who are still fighting the Christian battle on earth. The transition was instant. The Lamb has become our High Priest. The effect of that transition is significant to and for the Olympic Christian. The Old Testament sacrificial system of animal sacrifices and priestly representation met its conclusion when Jesus was sacrificed on the cross.

All of the cumulative sacrifices of the past were as promissory notes written in the hope that they could and would be cashed in at the bank of heaven. Had Jesus not suffered the indignity of crucifixion all of those former sacrifices would have been in vain. When Jesus died without spot or blemish a promissory note, as it were, was cashed in heaven.

The sacrifices and prayers of the past and a new era opened for sinners to have easier access to the throne room of grace. Jesus' death introduced two significant changes to every sinner's possibility for forgiveness and total emancipation. One; Because of his death, sinners no longer need to slaughter any animal as a sacrificial offering. His death covers all sinners. Two; The eradication of the old sacrificial system also saw the demise of the representational positions of the priests. Under the dispensation of the old system, sinners had to approach God through the priests. At the very moment of Jesus' death, the veil of the temple was ripped in two. *"And, behold, the veil f the temple was rent in twain from top to the bottom..."* (Matt 27:51).

The event of the rending of the veil was significant in many aspects:

- One: The veil was the divider between The Holy and The Most Holy compartments. It would have been blasphemous for any Jew to attempt such a separation.
- Two: The thickness of the fabric could not have been severed by the hands of man and the fact that the rend was from the top also signified that this was beyond the reach

of human hands.

- Three: Whereas in the past only designated priests were permitted to enter or even gaze into these holy compartments, the rending of the veil permitted the intrusion of any gazing eyes into these compartments without the consequence of spiritual retribution. This was, without doubt, an open and dramatic overturning of an old system and the introduction of a new and better one.
- Four: The old system now being overturned, sinners needed the assurance of adequate representation in heaven. This is when and where Jesus, the Lamb of God, made the transition from being the Lamb to being our High Priest.
- The fifth benefit of the rending of the veil is the benefit of the inauguration of a new system for sinners to secure personal forgiveness and absolution from their sins.

The sacrificial and representative system of the Old Testament gave way to the reality of a new individual approach. Whereas in the old system, sinners had to approach God through the ministry of the priest, the new system allows every sinner to approach God directly for him or herself. There is no longer a biblical mandate for sinners to confess their sins to any religious leader. Every sinner has the privilege and the privacy to approach the throne of God because of Jesus' death and because of His transition from Lamb to High Priest. Every sinner has the privilege and the privacy to approach the throne of God for him or herself. *"Seing then that we have a great high priest, that is passed into the heavens, Jesus the Son of God..... Let us therefore come boldly unto the throne of grace, that we may obtain mercy and find grace to help in time of need"* (Heb 4:14,16).

It is this transition to which the book of Hebrews seeks to draw our attention with the words: *"Therefore we ought to give the more earnest heed to the things which we have heard, lest at any time we should let them slip"* (Heb 2:1). The transition was made from Lamb to High Priest in order that He would become the captain of our salvation. With that transition being set in place Jesus commenced a new stage of His ministry that is beneficial to all who would pay attention and heed His invitation to accept His ministerial role and grasp the eternal opportunity to be with Him in heaven.

Indeed, the invitation admonishes new believers, (Olympic Christians) not to repeat the mistakes of past disbelievers. *"Harden not your hearts"* (Heb 3:15). The significance of the transition is further reinforced with the use of the word *"excellent."* Jesus our High Priest is positioned at the right hand of His Father in order that He would accomplish a more excellent ministry by becoming our mediator. The possibility for absolute excellence is due to His impeccable accomplishment as the Lamb of God which now qualifies Him as holy, harmless, and undefiled.

Whilst on a trip floating down the Rio Grande River in Jamaica, a British tourist pointed to the hills and asked the navigator of the raft;

"Is that where they grow it?"
"Grow what?" replied the navigator.
"You know" replied the tourist, *"grow the stuff."*

He was referring to the growth and trafficking of marijuana for which Jamaica is notorious.

"I don't know what you are talking about" replied the navigator.
"Anyway," replied the tourist, *"If you bring any of that stuff into my country, I am the man that you come to see."*

He was a judge who was on holiday for the purpose of being acquainted with the behaviour of Jamaican nationals. His knowledge would better equip him to be an adequate adjudicator of Jamaican nationals who violate the law by trafficking contraband within the United Kingdom.

In like manner, Jesus lived and mingled with sinners in order that He would be adequately acquainted with the feelings and infirmities of mankind. Therefore, when He assumed His position as our High Priest, he did so with a wealth of practical experience that is unquestionable. *"For we have not an High Priest which cannot be touched with the feeling of our infirmities; but was in all points tempted like as we are, yet without sin"* (Heb 4:15).

The supreme excellence of this transformation resides in the fact that in that singular sacrifice was concentrated all the accumulated sacrifices of the past and that it needed only to be accomplished once. Because of this singular accomplishment, He is considered to be truly great and perfect.

Moving on from the book of Hebrews, the reader's attention is drawn to a more vivid image of a renewed and transformed Lamb of God. Whilst the knowledge of His ministry as High Priest is admirable, there is a more vivid depiction of the transformation. As John the Revelator turned to see the person behind the voice that trumpeted in his ears, he was amazed to see the Jesus whom he knew, clothed in resplendent garments and ministering among the candlesticks. As a ministering servant and a humble Lamb on earth, there was no form or comeliness in him that we should desire, but now he is transformed, dressed in a manner that eclipsed the depiction of the aura of the earthly high priest – dressed for *"glory and for beauty."*

The reader's attention must be drawn to the impact of this vivid depiction.

- Full length garment that reached down to his feet.
- A golden girdle around his waist.
- Hair like wool and white as snow.
- Eyes as flames of fire.
- Feet like fine burnished brass.
- The voice as thunderous waters.
- Seven stars in his right hand.
- A sharp two edged sword proceeding from his mouth.
- His face shining with the strength of the sun.
- Stunningly colourful garments.

This vivid depiction is all in preparation for the grandest world event that is yet to come. The Lamb transformed and renewed is preparing for the final act of redemption. With the events of this world in utter chaos, one does not need to possess a degree in rocket science to conclude that the world is drawing to an end. Jesus, however, is making a final bid to save all who would avail themselves of this grand opportunity to join the Christian race. This is not a call for denominational affiliation; it is a call for every individual to position themselves for the anticipated return of the Lamb of God.

He will undoubtedly return, but the impact of His return will be significant to two groups of people. To one group who care nothing for the significance of warning messages that have been sent to them, His appearance will be sudden and unexpected.

Their unpreparedness and disappointment is depicted with the word; "*There shall be weeping and gnashing of teeth.*" To the other group there shall be joy unspeakable. "*So Christ was once offered to bear the sins of many; and unto them that look for him shall he appear the second time without sin unto salvation*" (Heb 9:28).

To those prepare and ready for His return there shall be joy. To those who are unprepared there shall be sorrow and bitterness.

Notes

1. M.L. Andreason, <u>The Sanctuary Service</u>.
    Review and Herald Publishing Association. Washington D.C. p:155

7 THE FINISH

Some may argue that taking part in the Olympics is all about the competition. Competing is truly a joy, but that joy is made all the sweeter when a medal award is the fruit of his/her labour. For many athletes several years of training and preparation are invested into securing the ultimate reward of their respective competition. Finishing the sport is what athletes prepare for and what spectators relish to see. It is the ultimate demonstration of speed, strength, agility, endurance or skill.

The thrill of the last moments of the competition is the demonstrative answer to the question; Who is the best? The sprint competitions appear to epitomise the climax of all the competitions. These have been immortalised by thrilling legendary performances from the likes of Jesse Owens, Michael Johnson, Florence Griffin Joiner and latterly, Usain Bolt. All legendary performers, but what about the competitors who attained fourth places and beyond?

The modern Olympics exclusively highlight the spectacular performers to the exclusion of the competitors who they left behind in the wake of their path to glory. In the conclusion of The Christian Race, however, this will not be the scenario. The Olympic Christian is guaranteed the assurance that when he or she has completed their race, he or she will receive notable accolades regardless of their finishing position in this monumental race. The greatest and wisest decision is to join the race and run, no matter what.

The Spectators

The obvious liability of those who sit in the spectator's gallery is their prohibition to physically assist the athletes or cast any obstacles in the way of their performance. The Christian race is being observed by four groups of spectators; unfallen angels, fallen angels, fellow Christian believers and non Christian believers. They are all spectators.

Since the tragic event of the fall of man from heaven, the angels of God have actively assisted as motivating agents to all who would join the Christian race. Angels are not permitted to do the work that a Christian must do for him or herself, but they are there to motivate, strengthen and equip. They may not be visible to the human eye, however, the Olympic Christian has this assurance that the angels of God encamp round about them that fear the Lord. Whilst their numbers cannot be specifically verified, the book of Revelation assures the Christian that the angelic heavenly host is numbered figuratively as ten thousand times ten thousand. These heavenly angels outnumber the fallen angels by at least two to one.

In a practical demonstration of the advantage that stands in favour and support of the Christian, the prophet Elisha prayed that the Lord may open the eyes of his servant to the host of innumerable angelic host that may surround the Christian at any given time. In response to the revelation that the prophet Elisha was able to disclose to the king of Israel every secret plot that the Syrian army had planned against Israel, the king instructed his army to locate and apprehend the prophet. Upon learning that the prophet was abiding in the town of Dothan, the Syrian army was deployed to surround the town at night. In the morning Elisha's servant was struck with consternation as his eyes were confronted with the surrounding army. Elisha responded with calm composure declaring; *"Fear not; for they that be with us are more than they that be with them"* (2Kg 6:16).

Given that his eyes could only see a host of Syrian soldiers, that was an incredible statement to hear. Elisha, however, went one step further and prayed that the Lord would open the eyes of his servant that he may see. Elisha's prayer was immediately answered. The eyes of his servant were immediately opened to a mountain surrounded with an army of heavenly angels with chariots of fire. This is the advantage that Christians have in their favour; an invisible arm that outnumbers and dwarfs the opposition. With that knowledge in mind, each person who joins the Christian race is assured of a cloud of witnesses that is superior in power and number.

In opposition to the heavenly host that is cheering the progress of the Olympic Christian are the fallen angels from heaven. It is the purpose of the fallen angels to hinder and obstruct the progress of everyone who enters the Christian race. Like the heavenly angels, they cannot directly intervene or interrupt, but they will intervene and interrupt by proxy. The devil and his angels second the services of unbelievers and use them to be stumbling block agents for the cause of the opposition. The earth is in the final stages of a race that has been running since the dawn of Eden. The devil knows that time is running out, therefore his agents of opposition are commissioned to work overtime. The reassuring factor for the Christian is the knowledge that they that are with us are more than they that are with them.

The visions of non-believers in the Christian race are as the vision of the servant of Elisha whose eyes were blind to the presence of a sizeable angelic host. The major portion of this world's residents do not declare any devoted commitment to the God of heaven, however, many who openly declare their non-commitment are heard using the name of God in jest or in profanity. There is a pervading universal ignorance about the nature and person of God. The main reason for spiritual ignorance is the lack of willingness or commitment to enquire or learn. The Bible and spiritual agents will not yield their understanding to overt spiritual pessimists. The concept that spiritual things are spiritually discerned means that spiritual understanding only avails itself to those whose minds are disposed to learning.

Whilst the percentage of non Christian human spectators are significantly larger in number than the Christian spectators, their eyes are still very much focussed on the progress and performance of the Christians. Effective Christianity is not all about direct witnessing. Christians are automatically thrust into the spotlight simply because of their declared spiritual allegiance. Spiritual declarations become the focus for non believers, however, the new believer becomes an object of spiritual analysis. The life of a Christian becomes automatically transposed as a book that is seen and read by all men. Thus, the Christian who becomes an unwitting object of spectation is challenged to run a race that presents itself as a model for the unbeliever to emulate.

The fourth category of witnesses is the Christian spectator. While travelling along a road that may be beset with many perilous circumstances, it is very heartening to know that you are not travelling alone. The book of Proverbs provide us with numerous fitting anecdotes such as; *"Iron sharpeneth iron"* (Pro 27:17). *"Two are better than one"* (Eccl 4:9). *"A threefold cord is not quickly broken"* (Eccl 4:12). Fellowship and companionship are sources of strength and encouragement to the Christian. The eleventh chapter of Hebrews is a hallmark of spiritual champions who have trod pathways of danger and adversity, yet had conquered victoriously. These are witnesses that we may carry with us along our journey even as we regularly assemble with fellow travellers. The wisdom of assembling ourselves with fellow believers is strongly admonished, especially as the end of all races is nigh.

The Reward

The thrill of a competitive finish is made more glorious when the preferred competitor is numbered within the elite top three finishers of the respective competition. As trite as it may appear, it is startlingly true, millions of pounds are spent to construct a stadium in order that an elite few may experience a fleeting moment of universal glory. As soon as competitors have completed their final event they have to get out of the way in order to make room for the next event. The next moment of glory for the top three finishers is experienced when they stand on the winner's podium.

Three individuals stand on a podium comprised of three tiers signifying the accomplishment of gold, silver, and bronze finishers. The winner is honoured to have his or her national anthem played, in national recognition of their accomplishment. The moments that follow are brief and fleeting. Medals of gold, silver and bronze are appropriately awarded along with a bouquet of flowers. The camera and media attention that follows may be brief or intense, depending on the perceived level of attraction to the viewing media audience. The names and accomplishments are significantly recorded in the annals of Olympic history and life goes on. There is hardly a mention of the other competitors who failed to achieve a medal. This cannot be compared to the rewards that await the Olympic Christian.

The Christian race is a race of life. Whether a person joins the race at the beginning of life or near the end of life, the results of a successful completion are the same. When a Christian finishes their race the response is one of satisfaction. The words of the Apostle Paul are significant for all finishers: "*I have fought a good fight, I have finished my course, I have kept the faith: Henceforth there is laid up for me a crown of righteousness…*" (2Tim 4:7,8). The immediate reward of the Olympic Christian is the satisfaction of knowing that his or her reward is secure and certain.

The next stage of the Christian's reward is the reward of mortal transformation. Time has not disrupted the dynamics of this reward. Since the death of Abel millions of saints have been resting in their graves awaiting the sound of Gabriel's trumpet and the voice of the eternal life giver. Those who have died prior to the second coming of Jesus will not precede the living into heaven. This is part of the uniqueness and the dynamics of this reward. Mortal transformation of the living and the dead will occur simultaneously.

There will be no dead bodies in heaven. Heaven is a place of life and righteousness. Therefore, sickness or death cannot enter its gates. Transformation for heaven must take place on earth prior to entry into heaven. The best that life can yield on this earth is tainted with corruption and nothing that is tainted with corruption can enter the kingdom of heaven. Therefore, in preparation for entry into the kingdom of heaven we all must be changed. *"For this corruptible must put on incorruption, and this mortal must put on immorality…"* (1Cor 15:51).

The speed and quality of the impending transformation is significant. Whilst the Olympian remains the same in body and may even deteriorate due to the rigour of their training, the Olympic Christian will experience transformation with instant impact. When the race has finished and the trumpet sounded, the transformation from mortal to immortality will be faster than the blink of the eye. The transformation will occur *"in a moment."* The transformation will literally occur in an infinitesimal particle of a second. The speed of change will be augmented by the quality of the change. Our Lord Jesus Christ *"shall change our vile body that it may be transformed like unto his glorious body…"* (Phil 3:21). Now that is something to shout about.

Jubilation, celebration and glorification will begin on earth. When the transformation of every Olympic Christian has taken place we will all rise together, to meet our Lord in the air. Consider the overwhelming jubilation of the Olympic Christians even before they reach the gates of heaven. There are twelve gates of entry into the kingdom of heaven, or the Holy City, as it is also known. God in his wisdom, goodness and grace, has made it possible for all manner of personalities to have access to his kingdom. We may not all agree and synchronise with each other on earth, but synchronisation must take place with God in order that total harmony reigns in heaven.

Whilst the Olympian has to return to their humble dwelling on earth, the Olympic Christian will be the recipient of palatial dwellings. The New Jerusalem is briefly described as a City of Gold with gates of pearls. If the most skilful architects could be appointed to design the city of their dreams none could come close to designing a city of grandeur that compares with the provision that our Lord has already made for every Christian. Seven star dwellings on earth are mere dumps in comparison to what awaits the Christian.

Other rewards that await the Christian are merely incidental to the greater life that also awaits. The Olympic Christian will receive a new name, new garments, new health, and new ambitions. The totality of the Christian's rewards cannot be described due to the insufficiency of that knowledge. Four broad categories of rewards are significant for the Christians consideration.

- There will be no more sickness; no need for doctors, hospitals, or funeral directors.
- There will be no more crime; no need for policemen or prisons.
- There will be no more wars; no need for armies or weapons of mass destruction, and no need for politicians.
- There will be no rent or mortgages. Free quality housing is assured for everyone.

These are merely the fringe benefits of being a finisher in the Christian race. Whether you are blessed with lightning speed, or blessed with limping endurance, be assured that there are no losers in the Christian race. If you would apply yourself to hold on till the end of your journey, there is a golden reward that awaits you.

Bibliography

Andreason, M.L. The Sanctuary Service.
    Review and Herald Publishing Association.
    Washington D.C.

Barnhart, Clarence L. Robert K. Barnhart. The World Book Dictionary.
    World Book, Inc.
    Chicago.

Blanco, Jack. J. The Clear Word. USA.

Body Guide. Powered by Adam. Adam.com

Feyerabend, Karl. Langenshedt's Pocket Hebrew Dictionary.
    Hodder and Stoughton.

Green, Jay. P. The Interlinear Bible. Hebrew-Greek-English.
    Hendrickson Publishers. Peabody.
    Massachusetts 01961-3473

Guyton, Arthur C. Textbook of Medical Psysiology.
    W.B.Saunders Company. Philadelphia.
    London. Toronto. Fifth Edition.

Holladay, William L. A Concise Hebrew and Aramaic Lexicon of the Old Testament.
    William B.Eardmans Publishing Company.
    Grand Rapids. Michigan.

Jemison, T.H. Christian Beliefs: Fundamental Biblical Teachings for
    Seventh-day Adventist College Classes.
    Pacific Press Publishing Association:

Jukes, Andrew. The Names of God.
    Kregel Publications.
    Grand Rapids. Michigan.

Lynthgoe, Jane E. The Meaning of Al Shadi (El Shaddai) in Ancient Hebrew.
    April 28: 2008. Ieue.org/profiles/blogs/20096.36

National Geographic. <u>The Brain</u>. www.Nationalgeographic.com

Nostos Hellenic Information Society UK, <u>Brief History of the Olympic Games.</u>

Rosenburg, Jenifer. <u>History of the Olympics</u>. About.com

Scolfield, C.I. Rev. <u>The Holy Bible. Authorized King James Version</u>.
    Oxford University Press.
    New York.

Snaith, Norman Henry. <u>Hebrew Old Testament</u>.
    The British and Foreign Bible Society

Smith, L. <u>How to Prepare for your next Competition</u>.
    Brian McKenzie's Successful # Coaching (ISSN 1745-7513),
    Issue 33. 2006.

PORTABLE COMMUNION SETS

Crystal: Totally transparent. Having the appearance of glass, this set allows you to see the interior contents of the vessel even when the set is closed.

Alabaster: This set features a unique opaque shield which provides a conservative camouflage for the interior vessels so that the contents remain invisible when the set is closed. When opened the interior reveals the same vessels that are visible in the Crystal Set.

These communion sets are made of solid Acrylic.

Each sets is supplied with:
- One Bottle
- One Stainless Steel Bowl & Plate.
- Four Acrylic Glasses
- Logo

Crystal Clear Ministries
PO Box 53802
London, UK SE25 9BT
www.doublepower.co.uk
Email: pcholder@hotmail.com
Tel: 07908 637059